WILBERFORCE WAY

(incorporating
Walking With Wilberforce)

by
John E. Eckersley

with
Mark Comer
Andrew Dawes
Nancy Eckersley
Alison Lewis
Daniel Savage
Terry Weston

© and Published by
John E. Eckersley 2007

ISBN 978 0 9535862 4 0

Printed by
The Max Design & Print Co., York, England

FOREWORD

TO CROSS THE WOLDS and plains between Hull and York is to travel to a destination you can see for many miles. And as a way of remembering William Wilberforce it is especially appropriate.

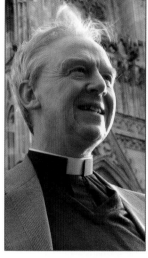

Photo: Martin Sheppard

To William Wilberforce, as Member of Parliament for Yorkshire for many years, this landscape was home. This is where he came from and in this place he was rooted as he served his country and the people of the world.

Motivated by his Christian faith, he saw his destination as the heavenly city in which the dignity of human life was incompatible with the treatment of other people as chattels. Walking towards York Minster is a fitting emblem of the God-inspired quest for a way of life on earth appropriate to God's intention for all humanity.

Walking is often a social activity and, as Wilberforce's achievement was the result of building alliances and trust with many people, so a walk across Yorkshire is a reminder of how much can be achieved by co-operation.

A walk with Wilberforce is therefore an act of love – for this region of England, for a great servant of the Christian Church, and for all those who still await liberation from slavery in today's world. Time to put our boots on again!

Keith Jones
Dean of York – 10th January 2007

INTRODUCTION TO THE WILBERFORCE WAY

In the summer of 2006 I was asked by Inderjit Bhogal to devise a walk linking Hull and Pocklington and to include this walk in the 2007 Wilberforce commemoration events. As investigations went on, it seemed sensible to extend the trail so that it finished at York Minster. Then just as I was about to hand the draft text to my printers, I heard that Alison Lewis had been preparing a heritage trail in Hull called 'Walking With Wilberforce'. This visits some of the key places with which Wilberforce was associated and Alison kindly agreed to include her walk in this present publication.

The **Wilberforce Way** is a 60 mile-long linear trail devised to mark the bicentenary of the 1807 Act of Parliament abolishing British involvement in the Transatlantic Slave Trade. This legislation was the culmination of years of determined campaigning by William Wilberforce and his fellow abolitionists. In one sense, therefore, the trail is a tribute to the pioneering work done by William Wilberforce. However, it is more than that. Today, two hundred years after the Act of Abolition was passed, it is estimated that there are at least 27 million men, women and children throughout the world still in slavery. So the trail also acts as a challenge for participants to become involved in today's campaign to abolish modern slavery in all its forms.

The **Wilberforce Way** starts in Hull (where William Wilberforce was born), goes through Pocklington (where he went to school) and finishes in York (where he was elected MP for the County of Yorkshire). This linear trail is divided into 13 separate but interconnected walks. As well as including locations of special importance in the struggle for human freedom and dignity, the 13 walks visit some delightful Wolds landscapes as well as places of more general interest. With one exception, each itinerary has at least one place of Christian worship along its route and so the **Wilberforce Way** can also be used as a pilgrimage walk.

It is possible to complete the **Wilberforce Way** using any of these different methods:

- as a single linear challenge walk of 60 miles
- as a staged linear walk with stopping points at approximately every 10, 15 or 20 miles
- as a series of 13 interconnected day walks
- as a single or a staged linear cycle ride.

The Ordnance Survey Maps covering the route are Landranger 107, 106, 105 and Explorer 294, 293, 290.

Travel information for walkers using public transport is available from The East Yorkshire bus company (telephone 01482 22 22 22) which provides express services (X46 and X47) along the A1079 road. Most of the day walks can be reached from this road. The A1079 also provides a helpful means of access for any support vehicles that may wish to accompany walkers along the route.

Tourist Information Centres at Hull (01482 223559/640852), Beverley (01482 391672) and York (01904 550099) can offer help if accommodation is required by those completing the route in stages.

Set All Free is a campaign to focus attention on the evils of modern slavery and to take action towards ending its abuses. It is hoped that this present book will help play a small part in drawing attention to the work of the Set All Free movement. The proceeds from the sale of the book will be used for helping Christian Aid's work of rescue and rehabilitation of those still trapped in slavery today.

WILBERFORCE WAY

CYCLE AND WALK DISTANCES

WALK LOCATIONS	WW DISTANCE (miles approx)	WW (TOTAL) (miles approx)	CIRCLE WALK (miles approx)	CYCLE ROUTE (miles approx)
1 THE DEEP - DUNSWELL	6.8	6.8	–	7.9
2 DUNSWELL - BEVERLEY MINSTER	4.0	10.8	10.1	5.0
3 BEVERLEY MINSTER - near CHERRY BURTON	3.7	14.5	12.0	6.2
4 near CHERRY BURTON - GARDHAM	4.1	18.6	7.5	3.5
5 GARDHAM - near GOODMANHAM	3.9	22.5	10.0	3.6
6 near GOODMANHAM - LONDESBOROUGH	5.0	27.5	7.9	5.6
7 LONDESBOROUGH - NUNBURNHOLME	2.6	30.1	5.1	2.8
8 NUNBURNHOLME - POCKLINGTON	5.1	35.2	9.3	4.3
9 POCKLINGTON - MELBOURNE INGS	6.2	41.4	11.7	5.5
10 MELBOURNE INGS - SUTTON UPON DERWENT . . .	4.6	46.0	10.4	3.7
11 SUTTON UPON DERWENT - near POOL BRIDGE . . .	7.0	53.0	–	7.0
12 near POOL BRIDGE - WALMGATE STRAY	4.3	57.3	9.2	5.2
13 WALMGATE STRAY - YORK MINSTER	3.2	60.5	8.0	2.8
Totals	–	60.5	101.2	63.1

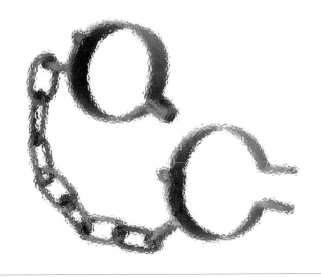

THE BACKGROUND TO 1807

Slavery – the word comes from 'slav' and referred to peoples enslaved in the Middle Ages in Eastern Europe – has existed for millennia in many different societies. But the Transatlantic Slave Trade was altogether more brutal than anything the world had previously experienced. The triangular trade meant ships from Europe took cheap goods to West Africa, traded them for slaves, carried the slaves to the New World, sold them for sugar, cotton and tobacco, and then returned to Europe with their cargoes. The transportation of slaves to the Americas had been started by the Portuguese and the Dutch and the first English slaving expedition is thought to have been that of Sir John Hawkins in 1562. By the late 18th century British traders took the greatest share of the traffic.

It is estimated that at least 9-12 million Africans were taken from Africa across the Atlantic as slaves between 1450 and 1850, enduring unspeakable conditions on the ships. On one occasion in 1781 over 100 African slaves were thrown overboard from the slave ship *Zong* in order to lighten the ship's load. Those who did actually reach the West Indies and North America were then subjected to dreadful conditions on the plantations. Some members of the Church were involved in slavery, even to the extent that one society allowed the branding of their slaves with a red-hot iron. Nevertheless, once the abolition campaign gained momentum, Christians were at the forefront. Today we look with disgust at the repugnance of this traffic but at the time it was accepted as part of what might be described as a 'cultural norm'. Many individuals in Britain benefited hugely from slavery and the prosperity of places like Liverpool and Bristol owed their wealth to the slave trade.

Yet slowly the tide of public opinion against slavery increased. The following were some key events in the campaign.

1780 William Wilberforce was elected MP for Hull, starting a parliamentary career lasting 53 years.

1784 He stood for, and won, the more influential seat of Yorkshire. It was at this time that Wilberforce became a committed Christian, a move that would radically influence his future life.

1787 The Society for the Abolition of the Slave Trade was founded with a committee composed mainly of dedicated Quakers. In the same year, Wilberforce met with Thomas Clarkson and later wrote in his diary; *'God Almighty has set before me two great objects: the suppression of the slave trade and the reformation of society.'*

1788 Wilberforce introduced his first anti-slavery motion into Parliament. He would do the same for the next 18 years because the opposition to his campaign was so entrenched.

1807 Eventually, on 22 February, the House of Commons voted by an overwhelming majority to abolish the slave trade. On 25 March the Slave Trade Abolition Bill became law.

1833 It took longer for slavery itself to be abolished throughout the British Empire but at last an estimated 800,000 men and women in Britain's overseas territories were set free. To placate the opposition, it was agreed that the plantation owners would receive £20 million compensation. William Wilberforce had given 53 years of his life to the abolition cause and he died just three days after seeing his efforts succeed.

It had required a monumental and sustained effort by Wilberforce and his co-abolitionists to change the whole public attitude towards slavery and the slave trade. It is the aim of the 'Set All Free' campaign of 2007 not just to celebrate the great achievement of 200 years ago but, perhaps more importantly, to effect a sea-change in public attitudes towards modern day slavery and to work unceasingly for its eradication. Wilberforce declared in Parliament in 1816: *'They charge me with fanaticism. If to be feelingly alive to the sufferings of my fellow-creatures is to be a fanatic, I am one of the most incurable fanatics ever permitted to be at large'.* We need more such fanatics today.

Wilberforce by Arthur Devis courtesy of Pocklington School

SLAVERY TODAY

'Slavery ... I didn't know about all these forms that existed. Generally people would not believe that it is possible under modern conditions. They would say 'No I think you are making it all up' because it's just too incredible.'

(Archbishop Desmond Tutu speaking in Hull)

Anti-Slavery International describes half a dozen types of present-day slavery:

Chattel slavery is what might be called the classic form of slavery in which people are still bought and sold as commodities. Often they are abducted from their homes, inherited or given away as gifts. Examples today are found in Sudan and Mauritania.

Debt bondage occurs when a person is 'bonded' or forced to work to pay back money loans. This is perhaps the most widespread form of modern slavery. Once trapped into debt bondage it is notoriously difficult to escape and inflated interest rates mean that debts can be inherited, passing from one generation to the next. Estimates suggest that 15-20 million people may be trapped in this kind of slavery today. It is particularly a problem in India, Pakistan, Nepal and Bangladesh.

Forced labour includes any work into which people are coerced under the threat of violence or other form of punishment. It takes various forms in the modern world. Forced labour is a global problem and although the largest numbers are in poorer countries, there are more than 350,000 in the industrialised world. In Burma (Myanmar) forced labour can be especially brutal. The SPDC regime targets minority tribal groups in a policy of systematic oppression. Even elderly people and pregnant women are forced to act as porters, carrying heavy loads of army ammunition. Others are made to act as human minesweepers, walking ahead of the army. Many have been killed or maimed in this way.

Human trafficking is the movement of people from one place to another either through force or by deception in order to exploit them. Families trapped in poverty may be tricked into leaving home by promises of work or a better life. Once taken, they can be ruthlessly exploited. Examples of this kind of enslavement include those lured into prostitution. Often the victims are young and become sex slaves. Sometimes they are sold by their poverty-stricken families to the traffickers. Sex slavery is a curse not only in Asia. In Europe there is increasing concern over the trafficking of young women from the former Soviet Union. In the USA the CIA estimates that as many as 50-60,000 girls and women may be brought in as sex slaves every year. Human trafficking is now so common that it is the third most profitable criminal activity in the world after illegal drugs and arms trafficking. A 2005 report by the United Nations estimates that there are 2.45 million people trafficked around the world each year – and that 50% are children.

Early and forced marriage, when women and girls are given no freedom to choose whom they marry, can be seen as another type of slavery. Women forced into marriage can face a life of servitude that is often marked by physical violence.

Child labour includes all those children that may be enslaved by any of the systems described above. Their physical vulnerability and lack of voice makes them especially prone to danger. An estimated 80 million children are trapped in the worst forms of child labour, with many more working full time at the expense of their education and development.

'No one shall be held in slavery or servitude; slavery and the slave trade shall be prohibited in all their forms.' (Article 4 United Nations Universal Declaration of Human Rights, 1948)

'At least 27 million men, women and children are slaves today' (Caroline Cox and John Marks, 2006)

*Pictured below: Child **Camel Jockey***

In 2004, Anti-Slavery International sent a photographer to the United Arab Emirates (UAE) to photograph children racing and training in the Gulf state. The photographs prove that, despite the Government's repeated statements that this practice has stopped, it is still a problem. Two years ago, the Government announced that using children under 15 and lighter than 45 kilograms to race camels would be banned from 1 September 2002 and offenders punished. All the photographs below were taken in 2004 at the Nad Al Sheba racecourse in Dubai, but children were seen racing and training across the country.

Photo: CDP/Anti-Slavery International

WILLIAM WILBERFORCE

'During the millennium year, there were several requests for people in public life to nominate the greatest Britons of the last 1,000 years. When I received such a request, I must say that I had not a moment's hesitation: William Wilberforce was my answer, because I can't think of any one Briton of the last millennium who has changed the lives of so many for the better.' (Archbishop Rowan Williams: Foreword to 'The Wilberforce Connection' by Clifford Hill)

The Wilberforce family were highly respected merchants of Hull where William's grandfather was twice Lord Mayor. William stood for parliament in 1780 at the age of only twenty-one. He was never a minister of the Crown but he became the moral voice of the House of Commons. He joined the Christian Evangelical movement and was a leading member of the Clapham sect. He gave away a quarter of his income annually and joined a number of organisations for promoting good causes or abolishing abuses which were a feature of late 18th century English life. Amongst the causes with which he was involved were police reform, better education for prisoners, free medical aid for the poor, education for deaf children, restriction on the use of child labour, action against gambling, establishment of the RSPCA, the foundation of the Church Missionary Society and the formation of the Bible Society. His greatest contribution, however, was to the movement to abolish slavery and the slave trade. The Committee for the Abolition of the Slave Trade was set up in 1787 and Wilberforce was its parliamentary leader. He undertook the task with great seriousness, chairing public meetings, writing pamphlets and giving his findings to the House of Commons. The opposition hardened. He was told that the slave-owners were doing the slaves a favour by rescuing them from 'the gross and impenetrable gloom of barbarism'; that the pleasant voyage from Africa was often the happiest time of their lives; that the future of British colonialism depended on the slave trade; and that, if he continued his campaign, there would be a rebellion in the West Indies and all the white settlers would be massacred.

In the House of Commons, every parliamentary device was used to defeat him. Bills went into committee, and never emerged. Others went untabled at the end of a parliamentary session, and so lapsed. There was a 'Great Debate' in 1792 in which the House grudgingly agreed to a motion that 'the slave trade ought to be *gradually* abolished' but that led to no action.

When England went to war with revolutionary France, the clarion calls of liberty, equality and fraternity could not be invoked and the Abolitionists were accused of being Jacobins and traitors. However, when the worst of the French Revolution was over, Wilberforce returned to the attack, annually proposing a motion for a Bill against the Slave trade. Annually, the Commons voted him down. At last in 1807, a Bill became law. Slavery still existed but the profitable slave trade had been stopped in England and the colonies.

Wilberforce turned his attention to the international scene. One of the terms of the Treaty of Vienna in 1815 obliged France to liberate slaves in the remaining French colonies over a five year period. Wilberforce worked incessantly, interviewing and answering an enormous correspondence. He continued to collect evidence of cruelty and moral degradation and to follow up individual cases. He and his colleagues incurred the full anger of the sugar-planters who blamed them for riots and insurrections.

Wilberforce worked for many causes but it is for his persistent work for the Anti-Slavery Movement that he is chiefly honoured.

(Reproduced by kind permission of Kathleen Jones: 'The Saints of the Anglican Calendar')

SOME OF THE OTHER ABOLITIONIST PERSONALITIES

William Wilberforce was the leader of the campaign to abolish the slave trade. But the movement involved many other men and women from different walks of life united in a common aim. Christians from a variety of denominations were at the forefront of the campaign. The following brief notes give an indication of the backgrounds of some of the other leaders.

Thomas Clarkson wrote an academic essay ('Is it lawful to make slaves of others against their will?') but was so appalled by his research findings that he determined to make the abolition of slavery his life's main aim. In 1787 he joined with Granville Sharp and others to form the Society for the Abolition of the Slave Trade. Clarkson knew that abolition would only come through Parliament and it was he who contacted William Wilberforce to convince him that he should spearhead the campaign. Clarkson was the movement's researcher; he is said to have interviewed some 20,000 sailors and amassed the evidence necessary for persuading the public of the inhumanity of slavery.

Granville Sharp saw a West Indian slave being savagely beaten by his master in London and was moved to take up the cause of the oppressed. It was Sharp's efforts that led to the landmark court ruling of 1772 that 'as soon as any slave sets foot upon English territory he becomes free'. This, 'the Somerset case' referring to the slave James Somerset, outlawed slavery in England and marked the first step in the long fight for abolition. Sharp spent his personal funds on behalf of slaves and was one of those who established Sierra Leone as a place of freedom for emancipated slaves.

Zachary Macaulay went to Jamaica as an estate manager when he was 16 years old. He returned horrified by his eye-witness experiences and was persuaded to go to Sierra Leone as first Governor to help in the resettling of freed slaves. When ill-health forced him to return to Britain, he chose to travel in a slave ship to empathise with the slaves. Macaulay worked as a researcher with an amazing attention to the detailed facts and figures behind the campaign.

Hannah More found her talents as a writer of great value when she joined the anti-slavery movement in 1776. She was a close friend of John Newton and her writings inspired many women to take action against slavery.

John Newton had a colourful life. Press-ganged into the navy in 1744, he managed to escape but was recaptured and then flogged. Almost drowning in an Atlantic storm, he found himself facing God and was saved by the Creator's 'amazing grace'. After becoming a slave ship captain, he eventually left the sea and opened his home for Bible study.

Then he was ordained, proved himself to be an outstanding Anglican preacher, and became active in the anti-slavery cause.

Olaudah Equiano, an African prince (above), survived being transported across the Atlantic as a slave and later managed to buy his freedom and sail back to London where he educated himself and became an associate of Granville Sharp. His autobiography gave Britons the opportunity to understand the evils of slavery from the perspective of one who had personally endured its torments. Olaudah's abolitionist activities were fully authentic.

Toussaint L'Ouverture led a slave rebellion in the West Indian territory of St Domingue (Haiti) in 1791. He enabled his slave army to defeat the French as well as the invading Spanish and British. He became, in practice, governor of the colony but in 1803 he was tricked by French forces, seized and taken to France. There he died in prison.

Sam Sharpe was a Baptist lay preacher in Jamaica and led a slave strike demanding that the plantation owners pay wages to the workers. When these demands were refused, the 'Christmas Rebellion' broke out in December 1831. Sam Sharpe was captured, then hanged the following year.

John Wesley wrote his last letter in 1791 to William Wilberforce encouraging him to persevere in God's strength in his life's mission. 'This morning,' wrote Wesley, 'I was struck ... that a man who has a black skin, being wronged or out-raged by a white man, can have no redress; it being a 'law' in our colonies that the oath of a black against a white goes for nothing. What villainy is this?'

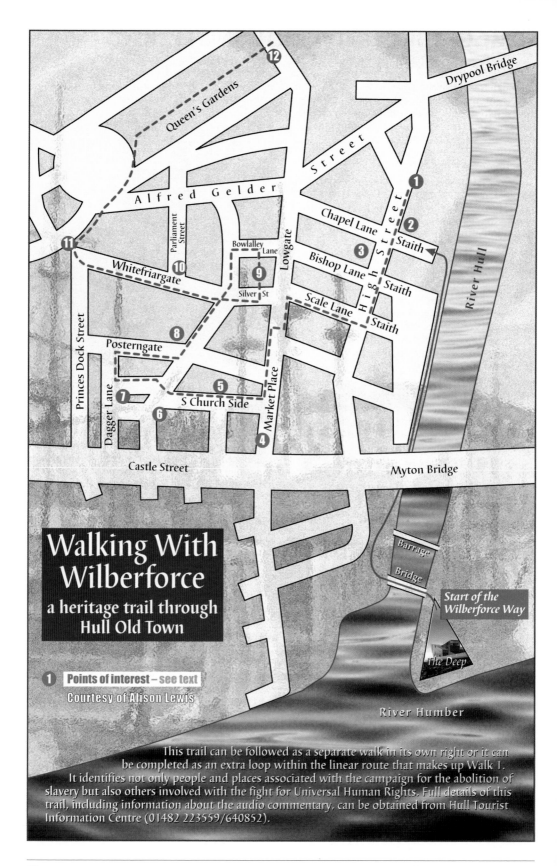

Walking With Wilberforce

a heritage trail through Hull Old Town

1 Points of interest – see text

Courtesy of Alison Lewis

This trail can be followed as a separate walk in its own right or it can be completed as an extra loop within the linear route that makes up Walk 1. It identifies not only people and places associated with the campaign for the abolition of slavery but also others involved with the fight for Universal Human Rights. Full details of this trail, including information about the audio commentary, can be obtained from Hull Tourist Information Centre (01482 223559/640852).

WALKING WITH WILBERFORCE –
a heritage trail through Hull Old Town

Assuming we are starting from The Deep and completing the full Wilberforce Way, we follow the bank of the River Hull to the Museums Quarter (see Walk 1), here turn left up to High Street and then right to **Wilberforce House (1)**. This marks the start of 'Walking With Wilberforce'. The House, now the Wilberforce Museum, is the birthplace of William Wilberforce and was the site of the family merchant and banking business. It was later the home of Thomas Thompson, MP, who was also a slavery abolition campaigner.

Opposite the museum was George Yard, the site of a former Methodist chapel where John Wesley is thought to have preached on three occasions. George Yard is today renamed Ghandi Way after the great Indian peace activist.

Behind us are the **Mandela Gardens (2)**, a place of tranquillity where we may pause for reflection. Nelson Mandela's reputation as an indefatigable campaigner for justice in his homeland of South Africa reminds us of the dogged persistence of William Wilberforce in his long battle against slavery in the British Empire. The biggest surprise in the Gardens is the highly imaginative '**Names on the Wall**' display – I'll say nothing more – just find it and reflect on the contributions that these men and women have made in the quest for the establishment of universal Human Rights. Adjacent to the Gardens is the **Transport Museum** which includes aspects of life at the time of Wilberforce.

Further down High Street we come to **Maister House (3)**, a fine example of the luxurious accommodation that the wealthy businessmen of the early 19th century might afford. We should make certain to look at the magnificent stairway, but also remember that while the rich could live in luxury, others nearby existed in squalor. As we proceed, we must make sure to peer into the alleys and staiths on our left leading to the old warehouses beside the River Hull. And can we spot the 1664 datestone on Crowle House, accessible in daytime on a gated staith near Bishop Lane Staith?

At Scale Lane we turn right and follow the cobbles to Lowgate and there turn left to the Market Place. Ahead of us astride his charger is the so-called '**Great Deliverer**' **(4)**, King William of Orange. The statue (1734) is a reminder of Hull's links with the Netherlands and would have been a feature of the market place at the time of Wilberforce.

On our right stands **Holy Trinity Church (5)** – note the inspiring reflections of the church in the Argos store façade - and it was here that William Wilberforce was baptised. It is the earliest major brick building in the country and further evidence of the city's link with the Netherlands. Rev. Joseph Milner ministered and preached here. Turning right down South Church Side, we can call in the church to see the baptismal font and a commemorative plaque to Wilberforce before coming to the **Old Grammar School (6)** that Wilberforce attended before he went to Pocklington. Here he was taught by Joseph Milner, whose brother Isaac was instrumental in leading Wilberforce towards accepting the values and beliefs of Evangelical Christianity. The old school is now a 'hands-on' museum. Carrying on straight ahead down Prince Street, we come to Dagger Lane, known locally as '**Nine Faith Lane**' **(7)** on account of the variety of worship traditions that was found in this area. This locality was adjacent to the Princes Dock and Hull was an important transit point through which an estimated 2.2 million transmigrants, especially Mormons, passed on their journey to Liverpool and thence across the Atlantic to North America. They were escaping poverty, famines and religious persecutions in the Baltic region.

When we reach Posterngate, we turn right, go past **Trinity House (8)**, built in 1753, and recall the importance of naval training in Hull's history. Then it's left along Trinity House Lane; straight through the Land of Green Ginger; right at Bowlalley Lane and right up the passageway to the **Old White Hart** pub **(9)**. This is the supposed site of the decision to defy King Charles I and therefore the place from where the English Civil War might be said to have started. If the time is right, it is possible to visit the 'plotting chamber'.

As we come out on to Silver Street, we go right and continue straight ahead along Whitefriargate and past the junction with **Parliament Street (10)**. When we get to the **Beverley Gate (11)** we are at the place where King Charles I was denied access to Hull. The remains of the gate and the former dock lock gates can be seen excavated below us.

Turning right, we cross the road to Queen's Gardens. This was the site of Hull's first enclosed dock (1778) but it was filled in during the 1930s. Today it provides a fine, traffic-free, green space in the city centre. We walk through the gardens, past the small Peace Enclosure, to the **Wilberforce Monument (12)** standing high in front of Hull College. This memorial was completed in 1834, just one year after the Abolition of Slavery Act and is one of the few non-military pillars in the country. Relocated in 1935 from a site near the Beverley Gate to its present position, the monument was paid for by public subscription. There is now only a short walk back to Wilberforce House.

WALK 1
THE DEEP, HULL - DUNSWELL

Map: Explorer 293
S.P.:   The Deep (103283)
Bus: Alight at Hull bus station (095291)
Wilberforce Way distance: **6.8 miles**
Circular walk:
     It is difficult to devise a satisfactory
     circular walk apart from the heritage
     trail through Hull Old Town
Special interest:
     Walking With Wilberforce heritage trail

The Wilberforce Way commences at The Deep on the River Humber waterfront at Kingston upon Hull. From here there is a fine panoramic view of the Humber as well as the opportunity to visit The Deep, claimed to be the world's only submarium.

We take the walkway over the River Hull estuary, bend right and follow the Trans Pennine Trail **pedestrian** signs. This permits us to walk immediately next to the river as far as the Museums Quarter where we turn left up to High Street. (Cyclists use Humber Street and High Street running parallel to the pedestrian route.) A quick out-and-back walk up Chapel Lane in front of us allows a visit to St Mary's Church, licensed in 1333 and Hull's oldest church. This is where the Wilberforce family worshipped.

It is hoped that those walking the Wilberforce Way will have allowed time also to include the Walking With Wilberforce urban trail described in the last couple of pages. However, for those

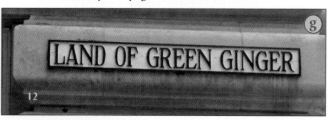

who are not sampling this extra treat, the Wilberforce Way continues northwards and, after passing the Mandela Gardens, brings us to Number 25 High Street, now the Wilberforce House Museum. Here is an opportunity to visit the birthplace of the man whose tireless efforts led to the abolition of the slave trade.

We continue along High Street to Drypool Bridge, cross the River Hull and carry on along the river bank following the Trans Pennine Trail fingerposts. When we get to North Bridge (1), we cross the road and turn right for a short distance to the road junction, turn left on to New Cleveland Street and then turn first right down Spyvee Street. This stretch of the walk can hardly be said to be inspiringly beautiful, but it does not last for long.

At the crossroads along Spyvee Street (2), we turn left and continue on the traffic-free cycle route. An underpass guides us right beneath the A1033 (3) and then just after going under the rail bridge (4) the path splits; we keep left until we come to the road at (5). Now we turn left and walk to the roundabout on the A1033. Directly behind the roundabout a set of concrete steps takes us back to the side of the River Hull.

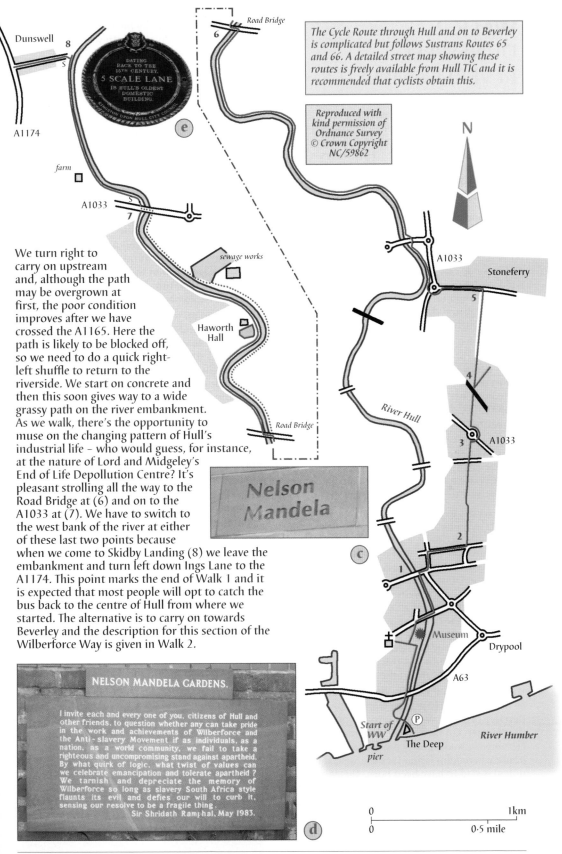

Dunswell

8

S

**DATING
BACK TO THE
16TH CENTURY,
5 SCALE LANE
IS HULL'S OLDEST
DOMESTIC
BUILDING.**

KINGSTON UPON HULL CITY COUNCIL

A1174

e

farm

A1033

S

7

6

Road Bridge

The Cycle Route through Hull and on to Beverley
is complicated but follows Sustrans Routes 65
and 66. A detailed street map showing these
routes is freely available from Hull TIC and it is
recommended that cyclists obtain this.

Reproduced with
kind permission of
Ordnance Survey
© Crown Copyright
NC/59862

N

A1033

Stoneferry

5

sewage works

Haworth
Hall

Road Bridge

River Hull

4

We turn right to
carry on upstream
and, although the path
may be overgrown at
first, the poor condition
improves after we have
crossed the A1165. Here the
path is likely to be blocked off,
so we need to do a quick right-
left shuffle to return to the
riverside. We start on concrete and
then this soon gives way to a wide
grassy path on the river embankment.
As we walk, there's the opportunity to
muse on the changing pattern of Hull's
industrial life – who would guess, for instance,
at the nature of Lord and Midgeley's
End of Life Depollution Centre? It's
pleasant strolling all the way to the
Road Bridge at (6) and on to the
A1033 at (7). We have to switch to
the west bank of the river at either
of these last two points because
when we come to Skidby Landing (8) we leave the
embankment and turn left down Ings Lane to the
A1174. This point marks the end of Walk 1 and it
is expected that most people will opt to catch the
bus back to the centre of Hull from where we
started. The alternative is to carry on towards
Beverley and the description for this section of the
Wilberforce Way is given in Walk 2.

Nelson
Mandela

c

3   A1033

2

1

Museum

Drypool

A63

NELSON MANDELA GARDENS.

I invite each and every one of you, citizens of Hull and
other friends, to question whether any can take pride
in the work and achievements of Wilberforce and
the Anti-slavery Movement if as individuals, as a
nation, as a world community, we fail to take a
righteous and uncompromising stand against apartheid.
By what quirk of logic, what twist of values can
we celebrate emancipation and tolerate apartheid?
We tarnish and depreciate the memory of
Wilberforce so long as slavery South Africa style
flaunts its evil and defies our will to curb it,
sensing our resolve to be a fragile thing.
Sir Shridath Ramphal, May 1983.

d

Start of
WW

P

The Deep

pier

River Humber

0 _____ 1km

0 _____ 0.5 mile

WALK 2
DUNSWELL –
BEVERLEY MINSTER

Map: Explorer 293
S.E.P.:   Ings Lane, Dunswell (074352)
Bus: 121, 246 to Ship Inn, Dunswell
Wilberforce Way distance: **4.0 miles**
Circular walk distance: **10.1 miles**
Special interest:
             Beverley Minster

This section of the Wilberforce Way continues from Dunswell to Beverley Minster and a circular walk is possible but the circuit does involve the potentially hazardous crossing of the railway and extreme care should be taken, especially if children are included in the party. There is plenty of room for car parking along Ings Lane in Dunswell and those using the bus (121 or 246) can alight by The Ship Inn on the A1174.

On leaving Ings Lane we turn right on to the A1174 and follow the road for approximately 1500 metres to the left hand bend near the Colletta and Tyson garden centre and Plaxton Bridge. (Alternatively, we may choose to use the concessionary route permitted by the landowner along the Beverley and Barmston Drain and shown (1) on the map.)

At the bridge (2) we leave the A1174 and take the path on the right-hand side of the Drain, cut in 1798. At Thearne Road Bridge (3) we carry straight on but at Ox Pasture Bridge (4) we need to cross over to the other side of the drain.

When we get to Figham Common, we enter one of Beverley's important Open Access areas and it's possible to choose a variety of paths. In dry conditions*, the suggested route is as follows: About 40m after passing next to Figham Bridge (5), Figham Drain comes in on our left and we take the path on the right-hand side of this ditch. A short way further on, we veer right and walk next to the trees along the left-hand edge of the open area. Where the boundary bends left at the end of a line of superb horse chestnuts (6), we need to turn left as well in order to come out at the kissing gate on the A1174.

Turning right on the main road, we walk as far as the B1230 and here turn left into Beverley. At Beverley Beck (7), we steer left and carry on to the Minster. On the way we note number 58 Flemingate, traditionally the site of an older house where John Fisher (see the Special Interest notes) is said to have been born. The Minster is the high point of today's walk and time should certainly be allowed for entering and reflecting on the importance of this superb building as a centre of Christian witness and worship.

We leave the Minster by the north door, walk round the west side, then turn west (right) on the B1230 towards Walkington. At Kitchen Lane (8) we turn off left and go past the allotments. About 50m after the right bend at (9), we must be sure to turn left in order to stay on a surprisingly attractive tree-lined path.

Crossing over the road, the meandering path soon becomes tarmacked and we follow the lampstands along the green corridor all the way to the second T-junction (10) where we turn right to stay along the edge of the suburban estate. At the children's play area, the p.r.o.w. turns right and so we walk round the edge of the field, then turn left and continue to Shepherd Lane.

Coming out on to the road, we turn left and go for just over a mile to where the road turns sharp left at (11). We go right for 70m on the track signed for Model Farm and Poplar Farm but then turn off left over the first stile. We now follow the field-side for some 300m (there should be delicious wild fruits in the hedge in autumn), cross the stile in the field corner and then take a very pleasant grassy path through a mixed deciduous wood plantation. With luck, we may see deer.

At the railway line (12) we curve right, continue under the A1079 and come to the ditch at (13). There is no official p.r.o.w. ahead to Lawns Farm, so the legal route turns right and follows the side of the huge arable field around to the corner of the electricity transmission complex at (14). Here we go left on the tarred track and soon turn left again, to pass Lawns Farm and its glasshouses. This brings us to the railway line. It is imperative to remember that the rail line is **not** a p.r.o.w. and that we cross at our own risk. On the other side of the railway, a quiet lane (which **is** a p.r.o.w.) brings us to Dunswell Road (15).

We bear left on the road, use the underpass beneath the A1079 and reach the bend at (16). Turning back left on ourselves, we take the

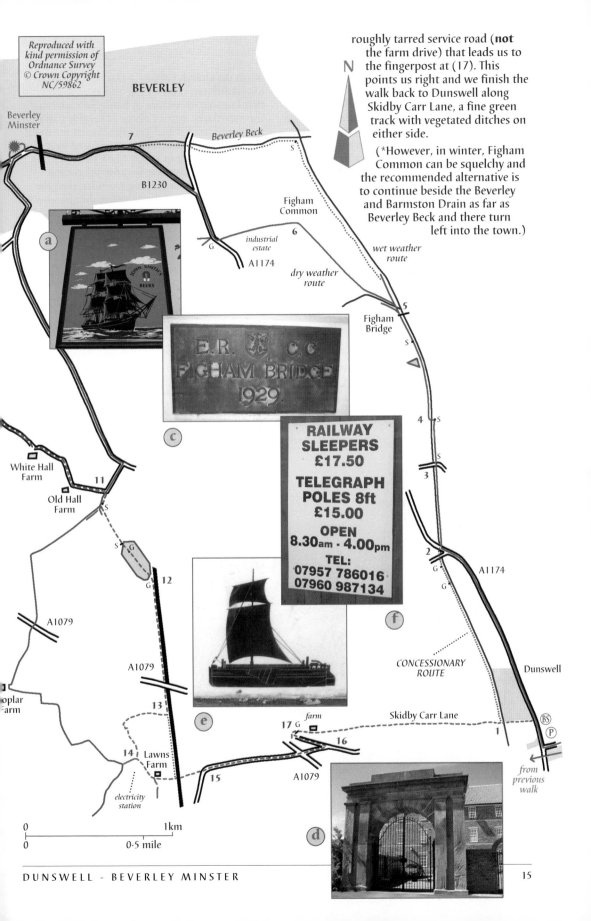

BEVERLEY

Beverley
Minster

7   Beverley Beck

B1230

Figham
Common

industrial
estate

A1174

dry weather
route

roughly tarred service road (**not**
the farm drive) that leads us to
the fingerpost at (17). This
points us right and we finish the
walk back to Dunswell along
Skidby Carr Lane, a fine green
track with vegetated ditches on
either side.

(*However, in winter, Figham
Common can be squelchy and
the recommended alternative is
to continue beside the Beverley
and Barmston Drain as far as
Beverley Beck and there turn
left into the town.)

N

wet weather
route

Figham
Bridge

E.R. C.C.
FIGHAM BRIDGE
1929.

**RAILWAY
SLEEPERS
£17.50

TELEGRAPH
POLES 8ft
£15.00

OPEN
8.30am - 4.00pm

TEL:
07957 786016
07960 987134**

White Hall
Farm

11

Old Hall
Farm

12

A1079

A1079

13

Poplar
Farm

CONCESSIONARY
ROUTE

Dunswell

A1174

Skidby Carr Lane

farm

17

16

14   Lawns
Farm

15

A1079

from
previous
walk

electricity
station

0   1km

0   0.5 mile

There are three Saint Johns who are closely linked with Beverley and we need to distinguish between them. **St John the Evangelist** wrote the Fourth Gospel and with St Martin shares the dedication of the Minster. **St John of Beverley** was born at Harpham and became a monk at Hilda's monastery at Whitby. Later he was made Bishop of Hexham and then of York. Whilst at York, he founded the monastery at Beverley and in his old age he retired there. Many miracles of healing were attributed to him, including curing a boy's inability to speak. **St John Fisher** (1469-1535) was born in Beverley and came to be a champion of the Church in the struggle against King Henry VIII. Henry condemned him to death and beheaded him.

Beverley Minster is wonderful. It gives the appearance of a cathedral because of its large size but it is actually a parish church. The building has seen many changes.

Firstly, about 700 AD, John of Beverley had a monastery built on a nearby site. After John's death the church became a place of pilgrimage. King Athelstan came in 937 and as a thanksgiving for victory in battle, he converted the monastery into a College of Secular Canons, richly endowed it and gave the church the Right of Sanctuary. This church was replaced by a Norman building in about 1170. However this edifice did not last long because the central tower collapsed. In helping to understand the present structure of the Minster, the guidebook suggests approximate building dates of 1220 for the East End, 1320 for the Nave and 1420 for the West End.

Partly because of its importance as a place of pilgrimage and also a place of sanctuary, the town of Beverley grew up adjacent to the Minster and by the 14th century Beverley had become a wealthy town, famous for its wool trade.

The guidebook gives a full account of all the items to find in the Church but for those walking the Wilberforce Way two things are of special interest. One is the **Frid Stool** or Sanctuary Chair. This is the only item remaining from the Saxon Church and, according to the inscription on the back, was originally a bishop's throne. However, when the Minster was granted the Right of Sanctuary in 937 it became the Sanctuary Chair. It was probably used by the Archbishop's officer who administered the oath sworn by the fugitive. He had to swear to be faithful to both Church and secular authorities and to promise to put out fires, quell strifes and carry no dagger.

Those who sought sanctuary were fugitives from the law and the list of those who came to Beverley is kept at the British Museum. Between 1478 and 1529 there were 469 cases recorded

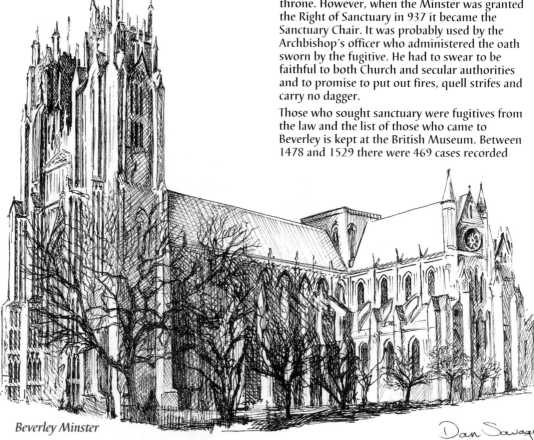

Beverley Minster

Dan Savage

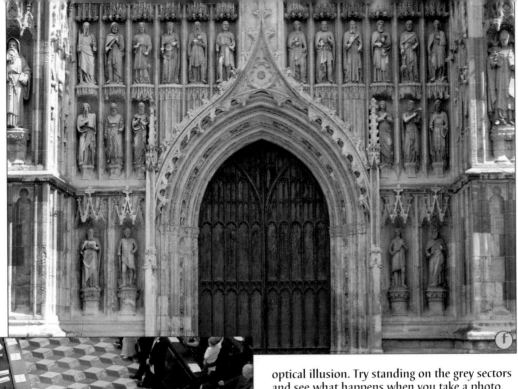

optical illusion. Try standing on the grey sectors and see what happens when you take a photo.

Visitors should also make time to see at least the following treasures:

- the tomb slab of St John of Beverley – the guide relates the story of the saint's bodily remains
- the Percy Tomb canopy - an exquisite piece of workmanship dating from around 1370. It is said to commemorate Lady Idonea of the Percy family
- the 68 misericords (hinged seats) in the Choir stalls – said to be the largest collection in England
- the late Norman font with its superb 18th century carved oak canopy
- the North Aisle stone carvings showing the playing of medieval instruments.

As well as spending time in the Minster, we should certainly try to see **Beverley Friary**, located next to the Minster and the only remaining example of a Dominican friary in the area.

Beverley Beck is recorded as being canalised and forming a navigable tidal waterway in medieval times. In 1802 a lock was constructed at the confluence with the River Hull and it then became possible to control the depth of the canal. The Beck played an important role in the growth of the town providing a vital link with the River Hull and the River Humber. Industries such as brick and tile making, pottery, cloth manufacture, tanning, corn milling and shipbuilding developed along the beckside area using the Beck for transport.

and the crimes ranged from debt and homicide to felony and coining. Hospitality was given to the fugitive for 30 days after which, if he had not reached a settlement with his pursuers, he was taken to the next county or to the coast to escape abroad.

As part of the Right of Sanctuary, crosses were erected around the outskirts of the town and these defined the limits of the sanctuary. The remains of three crosses survive and these can be seen at Bishop Burton, at Walkington and at Bentley, although they may have been removed from their original sites. The Right of Sanctuary was abolished in 1624.

The **Choir floor** (pictured above) is also of importance on the Wilberforce trail. Made of Italian marble, it was laid in the 18th century and an uncle of William Wilberforce is said to have been responsible for bringing the material to Britain. Attractive as the floor is in its own right, its distinctive pattern can present an

WALK 3
BEVERLEY MINSTER –
near CHERRY BURTON

Map: Explorer 293
S.E.P.:   Car park at Hudson Way (029414)
Bus: Alight at Beverley bus station
Wilberforce Way distance: **3.7 miles**
South loop walk distance: **6.0 miles**
North loop walk distance: **6.0 miles**
Special interest:
         St Mary's Church, Beverley town
         centre, The Westwood, Leconfield

From Beverley Minster the Wilberforce Way uses the Minster Way to the northern edge of the town and then turns W.N.W. along the Hudson Way rail trail. Walk 3 includes two distinct sections with a southern loop in Beverley and a northern loop going through Leconfield. A good start for those doing this figure-of-eight is from the centre of the walk at the free car park close to the beginning of the Hudson Way. However, for the benefit of those doing the linear walk, the route description begins from Beverley.

From the North Door of the Minster we walk down Highgate and come to the Wednesday Market. We carry on straight ahead down Butcher Row, fork left into Toll Gavel, go through the Saturday Market area, leave at the top left corner to go down North Bar Within and then leave the historic town centre through the North Bar (1). A quick look at the Westwood Byelaws down York Road to our left is well worthwhile before we continue out of town along North Bar Without.

We walk until we reach the sign for Bleach Yard Stables (2) and here we turn off right. The next half mile through suburban Beverley is a little complicated so some care is required. After

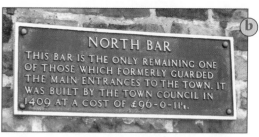

passing the cemetery on our left, the path goes through a small gate leading to the road called The Paddock. We turn left, then first right down Westfield Avenue. At the T-junction we go left but almost immediately turn right into Scrubwood Lane. Now it's first left down Oak Tree Drive, first right into Oak Tree Close and then left where the path squeezes between houses.

Fingerposts confirm that we are on the correct route and after crossing a small roundabout we continue to the gap between the houses at the end of Whitefield Close. We have now joined the Hudson Way and turn left (3). Then where the track divides we fork right to go over the footbridge above the main road. The Hudson Way then carries on ahead, though if we wish to use the car park, we double back sharp right.

Navigation over the next stretch gives no problem: we simply follow the old rail track, go under Driffield Road (A164) and come up on to Miles Lane at the trail access point (4).

On the road we turn left round the corner and walk for about 130m before going right on the drive to Rose Cottage Farm. The two fields on our right mark the site of the former village of Raventhorpe. Immediately before the farmstead, the p.r.o.w. turns abruptly left, then right, and so we do not need to go through the farmyard. When the tree line on our right finishes, we carry straight on a short way to the next hedge, turn left for about 100m and then go right through the gap. We follow the field edge for 70m, cross left over the ditch on a plank footbridge and continue to the field corner at (5). Staying by the ditch, we turn left and then come to the trees that mark the site of the former Leconfield Manor.

A right-left shuffle takes us along the right (east) side of the moated remains and at the next corner we leave the moat to go diagonally over grazing land to the stile in the opposite corner of the field. Three more stiles will bring us to the main A164 in Leconfield (6).

A short diversion to St Catherine's Church, signposted ahead and just to our left, is recommended before we continue on the footpath along the A164 towards Beverley. When we reach the end of the Normandy

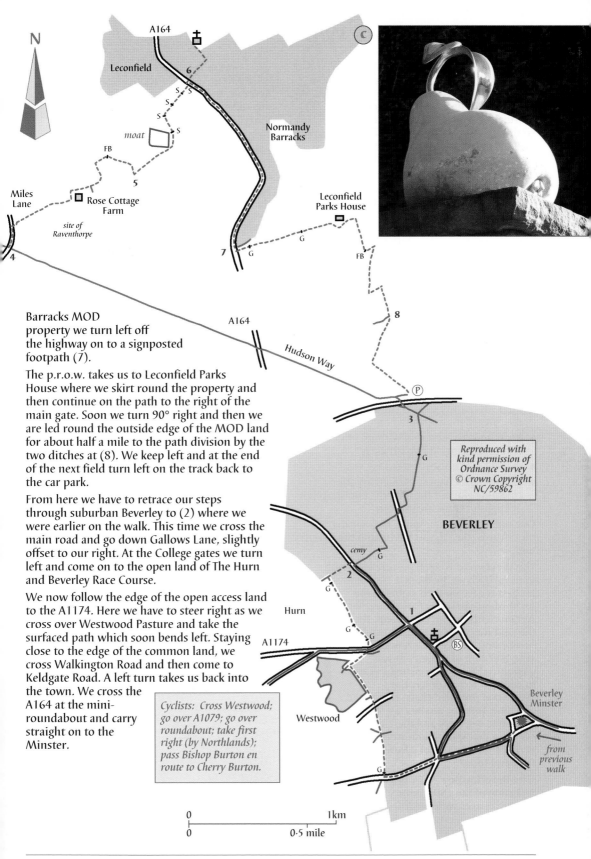

N

A164

Leconfield

6

S S
S S
S
moat S

FB

5

Miles
Lane

Rose Cottage
Farm

*site of
Raventhorpe*

4

Normandy
Barracks

Leconfield
Parks House

7   G   G

FB

8

A164

Hudson Way

Reproduced with
kind permission of
Ordnance Survey
© Crown Copyright
NC/59862

(P)

3   G

G

BEVERLEY

cemy   G

2
G

Hurn   1

G

A1174   G

BS

Westwood

Beverley
Minster

*from
previous
walk*

Barracks MOD property we turn left off the highway on to a signposted footpath (7).

The p.r.o.w. takes us to Leconfield Parks House where we skirt round the property and then continue on the path to the right of the main gate. Soon we turn 90° right and then we are led round the outside edge of the MOD land for about half a mile to the path division by the two ditches at (8). We keep left and at the end of the next field turn left on the track back to the car park.

From here we have to retrace our steps through suburban Beverley to (2) where we were earlier on the walk. This time we cross the main road and go down Gallows Lane, slightly offset to our right. At the College gates we turn left and come on to the open land of The Hurn and Beverley Race Course.

We now follow the edge of the open access land to the A1174. Here we have to steer right as we cross over Westwood Pasture and take the surfaced path which soon bends left. Staying close to the edge of the common land, we cross Walkington Road and then come to Keldgate Road. A left turn takes us back into the town. We cross the A164 at the mini-roundabout and carry straight on to the Minster.

Cyclists: Cross Westwood; go over A1079; go over roundabout; take first right (by Northlands); pass Bishop Burton en route to Cherry Burton.

0   1km
0   0·5 mile

Beverley has a fascinating historic centre and, if time allows, is ideal for leisurely exploration using one of the TIC's free town guide maps. We cannot avoid the glorious Market Cross (1712) bearing the arms of Queen Anne and when we go through the North Bar, rebuilt in 1409 and the only one of five former gateways left standing, we should be thankful that at least this one is still intact.

St Mary's Church is undoubtedly Beverley's most spectacular treasure after the Minster and it ranks high among the great Parish Churches of England. However, unlike the Minster, St Mary's owes its great architectural interest to the fact that it developed through nearly 400 years of almost continuous building, from about 1120 to 1530. Medieval music was important in the town and St Mary's was the centre of the North of England guild of minstrels.

Amongst a wealth of fascinating features at St Mary's, the following should certainly be admired:

- the 1530 font made of Derbyshire marble
- the minstrels' pillar (1524), the most important of some 34 musical carvings
- the 13th century Chapel (now Vestry) with the constellations painted on the ceiling
- the unique chancel roof with its 1445 timber ceiling showing 40 English kings
- the 600 roof bosses
- St Michael's Chapel (1325-1340), 'the crowning glory of the Church, a masterpiece of English Gothic architecture'.

Oh, and if you want a smile, look for the misericords, the Pilgrim Rabbit and the Beverley Imp.

The Westwood is open pasture land with unusual byelaws. In about 1258 the town burgesses gave up their rights in the Archbishop's Beverley Parks in exchange for certain rights on the Westwood. Then in 1380 the land was granted to the town by Archbishop Neville for a rent of £5 a year. Freedom of movement was guaranteed to all who visited the area. In addition to pasturage, the Westwood provided chalk, clay, wood and lime. **Burton Bushes**, an SSSI, has some fine oak trees and there is evidence that it is natural woodland, perhaps the remains of a former medieval forest.

'The Beverley Boy' story is a sad reflection of the 18th century attitude in which slaves were regarded as inheritable property. Thomas Ellinor (junior) was a bricklayer from Beverley who went to Jamaica. A copy of his will (1726) is held in the East Riding archives centre at Beverley. In his will, he gives his 'Negro slave boy called Beverley' to Edward Johnson of Kingston, Jamaica.

Leconfield is a place where the Percy family, Earls of Northumberland, had a manor house or castle, the large moated area of which still survives. A licence to crenellate (put up battlements) was granted in 1308 and early in the 16th century it was one of the main residences of Henry 'the Magnificent', fifth Earl of Northumberland. By the 1570s the house was in decay and in 1608-09 it was finally demolished, with much of the timber, painted glass and images being taken to Wressle Castle. Normandy Barracks, the former RAF Station, occupies the site of two of the three medieval deer parks linked to Leconfield Castle.

St Catherine's Church, Leconfield shows from the roadside a wonderful variety of building materials. What are thought to be the traces of a Saxon church are found on the outside of the building to the left of the porch. The Normans are likely to have extended the church and then later the north and south aisles were added. The tower was rebuilt and the porch added in 1684. Inside, the chancel was extensively rebuilt around 1860. In the middle of the 19th century the Lord of the Manor offered to build a new church, towards which he would give £1,000 – on condition that the villagers matched the sum with their own money. But the locals were unable to find the cash and so the old church with its fascinating designs remained. However, at the time of writing, St Catherine's is facing the very serious problem of dry rot and the flooring is undergoing major surgery. St Catherine's is notable for the graves of air force personnel from Leconfield who died in the Second World War. In the churchyard is the base of a medieval cross.

SPECIAL INTEREST - **WALK 4**

St Michael's Church, Cherry Burton was built in 1852-53 and replaced an earlier church on the same site. Cherry Burton Hall, is of late 18th century date but remodelled in the 1850s for David Burton, while Cherry Burton House was built by the rector Henry Ramsden on his private estate in 1829-30.

St Mary's Church, Etton dates from about 1150, has a list of rectors going back to1200 and has parish registers surviving, almost complete, from 1557 to the present day. Although the building was extensively restored and rebuilt in the 19th century, a number of fine Norman features remain. The church is therefore well worth visiting.

However, so far as the Wilberforce Way is concerned, the chief interest lies in the church's association with **John Lothropp** who was baptised here on 20 December 1584. John's story is an important reminder of the struggle for religious freedom and toleration four hundred years ago. Today many Americans regard him as one of their earliest spiritual leaders.

John Lothropp was ordained into the Church of England but during his early years in the Ministry he grew increasingly dissatisfied with the way the Established Church was operating. So he left the Church of England and became minister of the First Independent Church of London. Almost inevitably he came into conflict with the establishment authorities; he was arrested along with 42 members of his congregation and imprisoned. It was two years before they were released and then, in 1634, John Lothropp and his followers emigrated to the New World on board 'The Griffin'.

After a difficult first five years, the group settled at what is now Barnstaple, Cape Cod. Here a vibrant community grew up and when he died, John Lothropp's 12 children had produced families of their own. From them are descended a number of famous Americans including four Presidents: Ulysses Grant, Franklin Roosevelt, George Bush Senior and George Bush Junior.

The Hudson Way is named after the 19th century Yorkshire railway magnate who in 1847 opened a stretch of rail line from York to Market Weighton. Hudson wanted the line to continue to Beverley but the local landowner, Lord Hotham, would not at first allow access. He only agreed to a railway crossing his land on condition that a station was built at Kiplingcotes in order to serve his estate and so the extension to Beverley did not open till 1865. It survived for 100 years but, although it was profitable, Lord Beeching had it closed in 1965.

The section from Market Weighton to Beverley has since been developed as a recreational trail in memory of George Hudson, even though the entrepreneur was a somewhat controversial figure. He became one of the richest men in York, buying up more and more land in order to fulfil his railway ambitions. Eventually he came to hold 1,500 of the 5,000 miles of track in England. However, he over-stretched himself, fell into debt and as a result was forced to spend three months in York jail.

WALK 4
near CHERRY BURTON - GARDHAM

Map: Explorer 293
S.E.P.:   Road-track crossing (960428)
Bus: Service 142 daily
Wilberforce Way distance: **4.1 miles**
East loop walk distance: **2.9 miles**
West loop walk distance: **4.6 miles**
Special interest:
     Etton, Cherry Burton and the
     Hudson Way

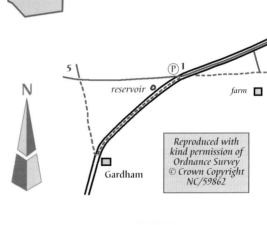

In planning this part of the Wilberforce Way it was decided to include the two villages of Cherry Burton and Etton on the actual trail. The slighter shorter, more direct route, along the Hudson Way is used to make the figure-of-eight day walk.

Parking is possible in either of the two villages, although the route description assumes we begin at the point where the Hudson Way crosses Gardham Road and where there is sufficient space for half a dozen cars. This means we complete the actual Wilberforce Way (through the villages) at the end of the walk.

From the unofficial car park (1) we take the Hudson Way eastwards for 2.6 miles to the Miles Lane access point at (2). Along the route we notice the remains of the old windmill (built around 1790) on our left just before New Road.

Coming up on to Miles Lane, we turn right, go past the golf club, cross the B1248 and enter Cherry Burton. As we walk through this Fair Trade village, we should visit St Michael's Church and study the village history notice board outside the school.

At the crossroads (3) at the end of the settlement, we turn right along Etton Road for a mile into Etton village (4). Here we must do a short diversion right to St Mary's Church, the place where the dissenting Anglican minister John Lothropp was baptised.

Coming out of the church, we can pause to read the information board by the road junction before continuing through the village along Main Street. When we leave

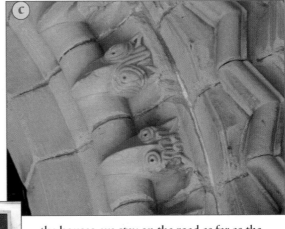

the houses, we stay on the road as far as the Hudson Way crossing point (1) from where we started the walk.

Now we leave the road and fork right for some 650m on the Hudson Way to the bridleway crossing at (5). A left turn leads us down to the road at Gardham and another left turn then takes us back to our cars.

THOMAS CARLING
(1797 - 1880)

Thomas Carling, youngest child of William and Margaret, was born and raised in Etton, Yorkshire.
He emigrated alone to Canada in 1818, settling near London, Ontario. He married there in 1820 to Margaret Routledge (1786 - 1871) of Cumberland, England. They had five sons, William, Thomas, Isaac, Allan and John, who was knighted by Queen Victoria in 1893 for his contributions to Canada, as both politician and Federal Cabinet Minister. About 1843, Thomas began brewing beer in London using his father's Yorkshire recipe. The Carling Brewing and Malting Company expanded throughout Canada and the U.S.A. and remained in the family for nearly 100 years.

Dedicated by Carling family members in Canada, 25 June, 2000

(f)

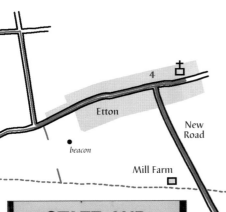

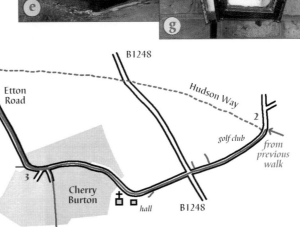

CHAPEL HOUSE

(g)

(e)

4 ☩

Etton

• *beacon*

New Road

Mill Farm ▫

B1248

Hudson Way

(2)

STAFF AND DELIVERY VEHICLES ONLY BEYOND THIS POINT

No children?

(b)

Etton Road

golf club

from previous walk

3

Cherry Burton ☩ ▫

hall

B1248

Cycle route from Bishop Burton

WALK 5
GARDHAM -
near GOODMANHAM

Map: Explorer 293 or 294
S.E.P.:   Kiplingcotes Station (929439)
Bus: X46 alight at Arras (926414)
Wilberforce Way distance: **3.9 miles**
East loop walk distance: **3.9 miles**
West loop walk distance: **6.1 miles**
Special interest:
       Kiplingcotes, Arras

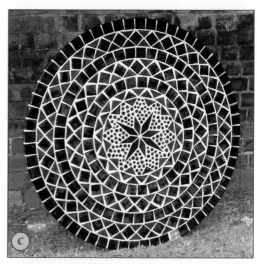

This section of the Wilberforce Way continues for nearly four miles along the Hudson Way from near Gardham to the edge of Goodmanham. However, for those doing a circular route, it's probably best to use the parking site half-way along the walk at the old Kiplingcotes railway station and then complete a figure-of-eight walk. The station is reached by driving from the A1079 down Kiplingcotes Lane and then following the signs for the car park. Bus access is at Arras at the junction of the A1079 with Kiplingcotes Lane.

From the car park we walk back down the access road to the crossroads at (1) and turn right towards Beverley. After a little over 0.5 mile we go right again at the next crossroads (2) and follow the road to the bridleway turn-off at the

end of Etton West Wood (3). Turning right once more, we soon reach the Hudson Way (4) where we were on Walk 4.

Turning right again, we stay on the Hudson Way and navigation poses no difficulty. As with other sections of the dismantled railway, this part of the walk is pleasantly green; nature has re-colonised and transformed the former industrial

Reproduced with kind permission of Ordnance Survey © Crown Copyright NC/59862

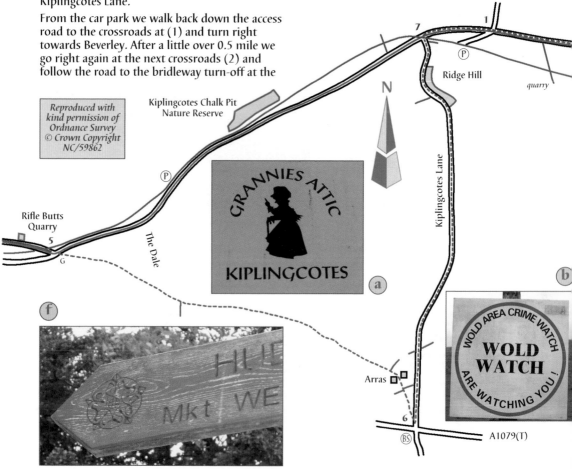

landscape into a very attractive environment. Soon after crossing the road to Wallis Grange we pass the disused Kiplingcotes Quarry on our left (look out for goldfinches) and then come back to the former railway station and car park from where we started. It's worth pausing here to study the information board before we carry on along the tree-lined Hudson Way.

A notice on the track-side reminds us that this section of the old line is classed as a linear nature reserve and after a mile or so we pass Kiplingcotes Chalk Pit on our right. There is no access at the eastern end but at the western end it is possible to go down into the former quarry if we have the time for a short detour. When we decide to move on, there's another mile along the Hudson Way to the road and the Wolds Way crossing at (5).

The circular walk now leaves the Hudson Way and, following the Wolds Way, turns sharp left on the road for about 150m to a T-junction. Crossing straight over, we leave the tarmac and, continuing on the Wolds Way, start to climb gently up the grassy slope. When we come to the top of the rise and the track begins to flatten out, we find ourselves traversing classic chalk

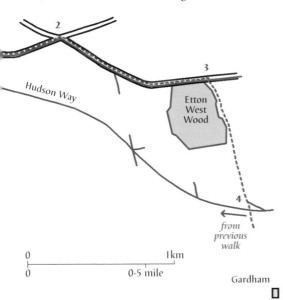

At this point we leave the Wolds Way, double back on ourselves and follow Kiplingcotes Lane for 1.75 miles back to the railway bridge at (7). The road bends sharp right immediately after passing under the bridge and then signposts direct us to Kiplingcotes Station.

Although walking on tarmac is not a walker's preferred choice of route, I was pleasantly surprised to see a buzzard on the roadside and there is an interesting variety of hedgerow vegetation along this quiet lane. In late summer and autumn time there is a colourful mixture of wild apples, hawthorn and wild rose hips as well as a plentiful supply of elderberries. If you are keen on wine-making, make sure you have a collecting bag with you.

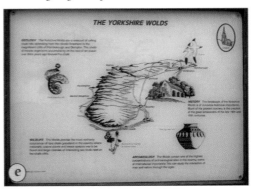

Wolds country, with rolling hills and steep-sided dry valleys, such as that of The Dale that we pass on our left. Certainly the open arable landscape with its broad views makes a marked contrast with the enclosed nature of the Hudson Way section of the walk.

Following the line of telegraph poles, we continue to Arras, the location of the renowned Iron Age burial site. Here the p.r.o.w. goes between the farm buildings and then along the sycamore-lined driveway to the main A1079 road at (6).

SPECIAL INTEREST - WALK 5

Kiplingcotes Chalk Pit SSSI is an important nature reserve managed by Yorkshire Wildlife Trust. Chalk was quarried from the pit from the 1860s when it was used for building the Market Weighton-Beverley railway. When the pit became disused in 1902 the exposed bare chalk formed an ideal habitat for pioneering chalk grassland species. Nationally, chalk grassland is an increasingly rare habitat and so it is important that sites like this one are protected and maintained. Some 500 species of flowering plants and animals are found; 250 types of invertebrate are known (including 16 species of butterfly) and 90 bird species have been recorded.

The bare chalk pit face is first colonised by mosses and lichens and these provide organic matter for the gradual formation of soil. This allows the eventual establishment of species such as basil, thyme, vetch and salad burnet. The floor of the quarry is floristically the most diverse and rabbits are a valuable aid in maintaining the variety of species because they provide areas of disturbed earth which pioneering plants can then colonise. Active management of the nature reserve is essential or the grassland would quickly 'scrub over' with plants like hawthorn and ash. This would destroy the chalk grassland habitat and so a programme of scrub control is necessary. This involves both cutting back the invasive shrubs and also using animals to graze the sides and bottom of the former quarry. Nevertheless, *some* scrub is left in order to provide a different kind of habitat.

East Yorkshire is famous for its **Iron Age burials**. Hundreds of these distinctive graves have been excavated and many more are thought to lie undisturbed below ground. The first major cemetery to be investigated, as long ago as 1815-17, was that at **Arras** and this site is recognised as being of major international importance. Lying about 0.25 mile S.W. of Arras, and now split by the A1079 road, was a burial area of over 100 small barrows. These have now been flattened by farming and there is virtually nothing for us to see on the ground.

The majority of the barrows covered simple graves, with brooches, armlets and beads, but three were probably those of chieftains, one of whom was a woman. These graves were more richly furnished and included the remains of chariots and horse harness and, in one case, the skeletons of the two ponies that had pulled the vehicle. 'Chariot burials' have since been excavated elsewhere on the Wolds.

One of the marks of the 'Arras Culture' is the distinctive square shape of the burial barrows and this feature is unique to East Yorkshire.

Tentative, and approximate, dates suggested for the Arras Culture are from the 5th century BC to around the time of the Roman invasion.

What is particularly fascinating is that elsewhere in the country, burials from this period are virtually unknown. On the other hand, the region does not have the traditional Iron Age hill-forts of this period that are characteristic of other areas. It seems that something out of the ordinary may have been occurring in East Yorkshire. One researcher* has noted that in very few cases are cemeteries found close to Iron Age settlement sites. It may have been, he suggests, that the Wolds were used for burial, not for permanent occupation, and that the bodies of the dead were brought from surrounding areas to be laid to rest in a landscape of the dead.

*C.Fenton-Thomas, The Forgotten Landscapes of the Yorkshire Wolds (Tempus, 2005)

Kiplingcotes Derby Horse Race was founded in 1619 and is the oldest endowed horse race in the country. The race always takes place on the third Thursday in March, starting from near the old railway station and finishing four miles to the north-west close to the site of the medieval village of Kipling Cotes. Allocation of prize money can be amusing. A very small fund exists and the race winner receives as his reward the 3% interest from this. However, the horse that comes second gets the majority of the entry fees. So if a reasonable number of horses enter the race, the second past the post stands to do far better for its owner than the first!

SPECIAL INTEREST - **WALK 6**

All Hallows Church, Goodmanham A wow church! The key can be obtained from Rectory Farm across the road and a detailed information leaflet explains why this site is of especial importance in the Christian history of Britain.

Goodmanham was the high shrine of pagan Northumbria when in A.D.625 Edwin became king. Making a political alliance, he married the Christian Princess Ethelburga of Kent but with the condition that she could bring her chaplain Paulinus with her. For two years Edwin pondered whether to accept his queen's faith and then in 627 he called his counsellors to his hall at Londesborough to consider the new religion. Paulinus spoke and the pagan high priest himself, Coifi, was converted. Seizing a war stallion and a war axe – both forbidden to him as a priest – he galloped to the sanctuary at Goodmanham, threw the weapon at the door and then proceeded to burn the shrine to the ground. A few days later, King Edwin with Ethelburga and his council left for York. There is a local tradition that it was at Pocklington that Edwin asked to be baptised but, whether it was there or at York, Edwin was baptised into the Christian Church on Easter Day. He gave Paulinus land on which to build a wooden church. It was soon replaced with a stone structure and, eventually, by York Minster.

It is not certain what happened at Goodmanham, though given its previous importance, it is likely that a church was erected here. The present building dates from around 1130 and a new millennium window shows scenes from its past history. One of the fonts, possibly of Norman age, was rescued from a farmyard. The other is perhaps the most highly decorated of any in East Yorkshire.

All Saints Church, Market Weighton has, according to Pevsner, some masonry that suggests it was first constructed in the late 11th century and the font is very old, possibly of Saxon date. There is a plaque in the church in honour of Sarah Andrews. She was the daughter of a Market Weighton shoemaker and was baptised here in 1774. She married Francisco de Miranda, the South American freedom fighter who later became Venezuela's first dictator. He died in a Spanish prison cell. Sarah returned to London where she died in 1847 and ended up being buried in a pauper's grave. Her memorial was unveiled by the Venezuelan Ambassador in 1981.

William Bradley (1787-1820) is reputed to be the tallest Englishmen ever recorded and his memorial plaque is on the wall of the house where he lived. He grew to 7' 9" and weighed 27 stones. William made money as a fairground freak, appearing in numerous towns throughout the country. On his death, it is believed he was buried secretly in order to avoid body-snatchers, who would have demanded a high price for such a large corpse. William Bradley was later re-buried in All Saints Church. In 2005 the local Civic Society created the Giant Bradley Heritage Trail in his memory.

Rifle Butts Quarry SSSI is of national importance on account of its geological interest. The succession of rocks exposed in the quarry starts at ground level with brown mudrock of the early Jurassic Age. Resting on top is a thin band of Cretaceous red chalk and above that the younger greyish-white chalk. What makes the site so interesting is the 'unconformity' or break between the mudrock and the red chalk because this division represents some 80 million years. During that time the sediments that had been deposited on the mudrocks were all removed by erosion.

WALK 6
near GOODMANHAM – MARKET WEIGHTON – LONDESBOROUGH

Map: Explorer 294
S.E.P.: All Saints Church, Londesborough
(868454)

Bus: X46 to Methodist Church,
Market Weighton (878418)
Wilberforce Way distance: **5.0 miles**
Circular walk distance: **7.9 miles**
Special interest:
Three Churches, Londesborough
Park, Rifle Butts Quarry

The linear route of the Wilberforce Way continues from the crossing point (4) on the Hudson Way that we reached on Walk 5. It follows the minor road into Goodmanham, passes All Hallows Church and then continues on the road towards Market Weighton. At the road junction by Mill House, it turns left, continues for some 200m, then descends left to the Hudson Way below the road bridge (5) before carrying on into Market Weighton.

However, the route description for the circular walk assumes we start from All Saints Church, Londesborough. We walk north-east through Londesborough village, past the information board, to the end of the houses and then bend down right on the signposted Wolds Way route into Londesborough deer park. When the Wolds Way splits (1) we fork left but the track soon divides again and this time we bear right and continue down to cross The Lake. Then the path rises gently through the parkland to meet a broad track at (2) and here we turn right and continue to the A614. Crossing over and veering slightly left, we pass the Towthorpe Corner picnic site to

our right and carry on along the wide farm track ahead of us.

The route is clear; we turn sharp left where the track is blocked and then swing right beside a tree-lined beck as we approach Goodmanham. Soon after passing under the old railway bridge the path divides; we stay left and enter the village. All Hallows Church is on our right and really should be visited before we turn left (E.N.E.) up the road. Just past Manor Farm the road splits and we fork right (3). (Anyone completing the Wilberforce Way as a linear route will be doing this section in the opposite direction.) The road takes us down to the crossing with the Hudson Way (4) and so links up with Walk 5 but just before this we should not miss visiting Rifle Butts Quarry on our left.

Turning right, we follow the Hudson Way for 1.5 miles into Market Weighton. Today the dismantled rail track forms a very attractive green corridor with Mill Beck occasionally visible through the trees down on our right. At the end of the trackway, we

follow the Wolds Way fingerpost directing us left into Station Road and this brings us directly to All Saints Church.

At the front of the Church we turn right on the road called Market Place and walk to the Methodist Church by the main road junction. Across the road we mustn't miss the wall plaque explaining the reason for Market Weighton's claim to national fame before we continue right along York Road.

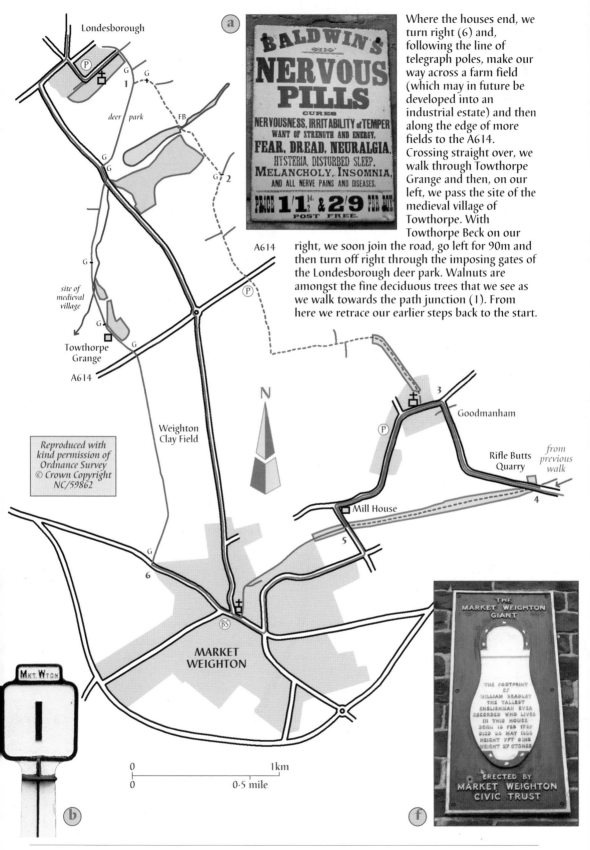

Where the houses end, we turn right (6) and, following the line of telegraph poles, make our way across a farm field (which may in future be developed into an industrial estate) and then along the edge of more fields to the A614. Crossing straight over, we walk through Towthorpe Grange and then, on our left, we pass the site of the medieval village of Towthorpe. With Towthorpe Beck on our right, we soon join the road, go left for 90m and then turn off right through the imposing gates of the Londesborough deer park. Walnuts are amongst the fine deciduous trees that we see as we walk towards the path junction (1). From here we retrace our earlier steps back to the start.

Londesborough

deer park

A614

site of medieval village

Towthorpe Grange

A614

Weighton Clay Field

Reproduced with kind permission of Ordnance Survey © Crown Copyright NC/59862

Goodmanham

Rifle Butts Quarry

from previous walk

Mill House

MARKET WEIGHTON

N

BALDWIN'S NERVOUS PILLS
CURES
NERVOUSNESS, IRRITABILITY of TEMPER WANT of STRENGTH and ENERGY, FEAR, DREAD, NEURALGIA, HYSTERIA, DISTURBED SLEEP, MELANCHOLY, INSOMNIA, AND ALL NERVE PAINS AND DISEASES.
PRICE 1/1½ & 2/9 PER BOX
POST FREE.

THE MARKET WEIGHTON GIANT

THE FOOTPRINT OF WILLIAM BRADLEY THE TALLEST ENGLISHMAN EVER RECORDED WHO LIVED IN THIS HOUSE BORN 10 FEB 1787 DIED 30 MAY 1820 HEIGHT 7FT 9INS WEIGHT 27 STONES

ERECTED BY MARKET WEIGHTON CIVIC TRUST

MKT. WTON

0   1km
0   0.5 mile

WALK 7
LONDESBOROUGH - NUNBURNHOLME

Map: Explorer 294
S.E.P.:   All Saints Church, Londesborough
                                              (868454)

Bus: There is no bus to Londesborough
Wilberforce Way distance: **2.6 miles**
Circular walk distance: **5.1 miles**
Special interest:
         Londesborough, Nunburnholme

As this is a relatively short circuit, it's possible to combine it with the previous walk and if we decide to do this, we can still park in Londesborough and complete a figure-of-eight walk. Those relying on public transport need to do both walks together, using the bus to Market Weighton. Although much of the route is on tarmac, the roads are quiet, there is a decent

grass verge and there are splendid views across the Vale of York.

Leaving Londesborough in the opposite direction to that taken on Walk 6 we turn right at the end of the main street and walk up to the crossroads at (1). Going straight over and following the sign for Burnby, we must not miss the panorama painting by the seat a little way ahead on our right.

Map

Nunburnholme

Reproduced with kind permission of Ordnance Survey © Crown Copyright NC/59862

Nunburnholme Hill

Cycle route goes this way in order to visit St James' Church

circular walk goes this way

Thorns Wood

Partridge Hall

Cleaving Coombe

Londesborough Hill

If cyclists choose this road they miss Nunburnholme

viewpoint

Londesborough

from previous walk

0   1km
0   0.5 mile

YORKSHIRE ASSOCIATION OF
CHANGE RINGERS.
St JAMES CHURCH, NUNBURNHOLME.
ON JUNE 7TH 1947
A PEAL OF MINOR, 5040 CHANGES
BEING 2 720's EACH OF OXFORD & KENT
TREBLE BOB & 3 720's OF PLAIN BOB
WAS RUNG IN 3 HOURS & 6 MINUTES BY THE
UNDERMENTIONED BEVERLEY & DISTRICT MEMBERS

FRANK BRAITHWAITE   TREBLE
CLEMENT GLENN   2
GEORGE DOWLING   3
JOHN HOBSON   4
LEONARD RODMELL   5
FRED OSGERBY   TENOR
CONDUCTED BY - LEONARD RODMELL.

THIS WAS THE 1st PEAL RUNG ON THE BELLS
RUNG AS AN APPRECIATION OF 50 YEARS DEVOTED SERVICE
TO THIS CHURCH BY Mr F. WILKINSON, TOWER MASTER.
CANON T.N. LAYNG, M.A., C.B.E., M.C. RECTOR.
A. YOUNG.   } CHURCHWARDENS
A.A. KEELING.   }

Then it's about a mile to the road T-junction at (2) where we do a right-left manoeuvre and turn down the track to Partridge Hall. Here the waymarked p.r.o.w. does a sharp left-right turn between the buildings and then we pick up a wide farm track. The route is obvious as we

continue past Thorns Wood, but after we turn left at the path junction (3) we have to keep to the right-hand edge of the field (and not use the obvious farm track) or we will miss the footbridge over Nunburnholme Beck. A short way beyond the beck we come to the road. About 200m to our left lies St James' Church and we can do a short out-and-back diversion now to see this architectural gem or, alternatively, leave the visit to the next walk. The key is obtained from Rose Cotage across the road. Close to the church is an information board outlining the history of the village.

We go north-east through the village to the end of the houses and here the road swings right and starts to climb back towards Londesborough. Nunburnholme Hill is a bit of a punishment at the end of the day but, if you can raise your eyes from the tarmac, there are some great views over the Vale of York to our right. By the time we come to the crossroads (4) it's all downhill into Londesborough but on the way we should take just a quick peek at the fine Cleaving Coombe dry valley on our right. Cleaving is the site of another disappeared village.

SPECIAL INTEREST - **WALK 7**

Londesborough, standing on the line of the Roman road from Lincoln through Goodmanham to Malton, is a fine example of an East Yorkshire estate village. It has been owned by a succession of wealthy landed families: the Cliffords, Earls of Cumberland; the Boyles, Earls of Burlington; the Cavendishes, Dukes of Devonshire and the Denisons, Earls of Londesborough who sold the estate in 1923. It was the Boyle family (1643-1753) who were responsible for landscaping the deer park, constructing the deer shelters and building the almshouses for twelve elderly local people. In terms of landscaping, the park represented an important transition in estate layout between the formal and natural styles. Straight avenues of walnut and turkey oak, some of which are seen on our circular walk, radiated from the Hall but this formality was broken by planting clumps of trees and digging a series of irregular lakes.

Londesborough Hall was demolished in 1818 and replaced in 1839 by the stately house, built as a shooting box, called Londesborough Park. Shooting parties staying at Londesborough have included royal guests such as King Edward VII. On Top Street is the village Concert Hall with the attached house built in 1880 as a laundry for the visiting Edward, Prince of Wales.

All Saints Church has a Norman south doorway above which is a 10th century Anglo-Danish Cross and sundial. The porch was added in 1678-9.

Nunburnholme lies at the entrance to a small valley cut into Wolds and its unfailing water supply and sheltered position have attracted settlers from early times. Stone tools found in the locality suggest evidence of Mesolithic and Neolithic activity. Later Bronze Age burial mounds and an Iron Age cemetery have also been identified above the village. Foundations of what is thought to have been a Roman villa have been excavated and in the late 12th century the Benedictine nunnery of St Mary was founded. Sadly only some earthworks and the site of its fish ponds now remain.

St James' Church is renowned for its superb Anglo-Saxon Cross which was found built into the walls of the church during extensive restoration in the 1870s. The existence of the Cross lends support to the belief that a church stood on the site long before the present building. It is notable both as a work of art and as a document of religious beliefs and ideas during the later Saxon period.

It may originally have been placed outside the church as a visual aid explaining the essentials of the Christian faith to a population that was largely unable to read or write. Ironically, the two halves were fitted back together incorrectly! An explanation of the carvings on the Cross is given in the church information leaflet.

The other main architectural treasure is the fine Norman tower arch dating from around 1100 to 1140. The Norman Church also still retains its nave walls and a small window but the eastern end apse which is thought to have existed was probably removed in the 13th century when the present chancel was built. St James' font is likely to date from the 13th century and the registers are complete from 1586.

Francis Morris, Nunburnholme's well-known 19th century rector, was a pioneer ornithologist and his efforts were instrumental in leading to the creation of the R.S.P.B. One of the bells given to the church in his memory but dedicated to St Francis has the inscription 'I will always imitate your birds, Francis, by singing' – an allusion to both the saint and the rector.

IN
MEMORY OF
THOMAS PELLING,
Burton Stather, Lincolnshire,
commonly called 'The Flying Man',
who was killed against the Battlement of
Ye Choir when coming down the rope from
the Steeple of this Church.
This Fatal Accident happened on the
10TH of April, he was buried on the
16TH of April, 1733,
exactly under the place where he died.

known to have lived in Pocklington for about 400 years. It is thought the cross-head was purposely buried during the Civil War in order to prevent it being completely destroyed by the Puritans. Then it was accidentally rediscovered in 1835 by the gravedigger. The cross-head was brought inside the church and mounted on a new column and plinth. An inscription was added to the plinth, linking the cross to the foundation of the church in Pocklington by St Paulinus in AD 627. In 2005 it was decided to display the original head inside the church and to re-erect the Victorian plinth and column, with a newly carved head, in what may have been its original position as a preaching cross outside the building.

At the other end of the church, on the outside wall, is the sad memorial to **Thomas Pelling**, the 'Flying Man', who was killed in 1733.

St Giles Church, Burnby is thought to have been built soon after the Norman conquest but the first documentary reference dates from 1288. In common with other churches, the Norman font was removed from the building and had to be rescued from a farmyard before it could be replaced on its original pedestal. Dedicated to St Giles, the patron saint of beggars, cripples and lepers, the Norman church has been altered and restored on many occasions. One 20th century problem the building experienced was the heavy

Burnby Hall Gardens is said to have Europe's largest collection of hardy water lilies in a natural setting. Percy Stewart and his wife travelled the world in the days of the Big Game hunters and brought back with them the trophies of their shooting safaris. However, it is the 45 varieties of water lilies that Percy Stewart left which attract thousands of visitors to Burnby Hall each year.

Wilberfoss village lies four miles west of Pocklington and has a interesting link with the Wilberforce family. By 1174 Ilgerus de Eggleton had acquired the Manor of Wilberfoss and, taking his name from the village, he became Ilgerus de Wilberfoss with lands stretching from Sutton upon Derwent to Stamford Bridge. Successive generations of the family lived in the village until the 18th century. However, about 1550, Thomas Wilberfosse married and moved to Beverley. This younger branch of the family flourished in Beverley and Hull. One of Thomas' direct descendants, William, became twice Mayor of Hull and began to spell the name as 'Wilberforce'. It was his grandson, also called William, who was born in 1759 and who was destined to become the best known descendant of the family.

All Saints Church, Pocklington is largely of 12th-13th century date with a few reused carved Norman stones in the porch. In 1835 a beautiful 15th century cross-head on a later shaft was found buried in the churchyard. It is called the Sotheby Cross and the Sotheby family is

weight of the York stone roofing slabs; these had to be replaced by lighter weight Cornish slates.

WALK 8
NUNBURNHOLME - POCKLINGTON

Map:	Explorer 294
S.E.P.:	West Green car park (801488)
Bus:	X46 to Pocklington bus station (803488)
Wilberforce Way distance:	**5.1 miles**
Circular walk distance:	**9.3 miles**

Special interest:
Pocklington School, Pocklington, Burnby Hall Gardens, Burnby

Pocklington is the place where William Wilberforce spent much of his school time and the circular walk starts and finishes at the free car park adjacent to Pocklington School. Although

square, we aim for the signposted p.r.o.w. leading between houses in the far left corner. This takes us past Bloomsbury Cottage and then round to the minor road (1) by the Sports Centre. Turning right, our route now follows the road south-eastwards for about 2.5 miles to Burnby.

There are a couple of places where we can leave the road, at least temporarily. At the end of the cricket club (2), for example, the Woodland Trust allows us to walk just inside Primrose Wood, parallel to the road, until we emerge a short distance further on. Then immediately after the sharp right bend at (3), we can take the path through the trees for a little way along the old railway line on our left.

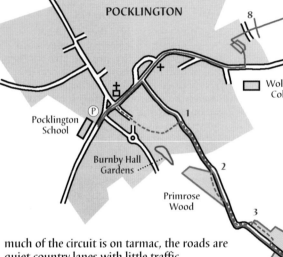

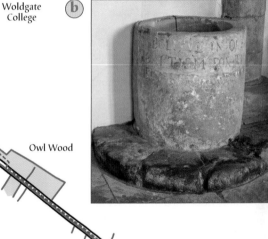

much of the circuit is on tarmac, the roads are quiet country lanes with little traffic.

Leaving the car park we turn left to the roundabout, cross straight over into Railway Street and then turn first right down Regent Street. Where the street opens out to a small

However, by the time we reach the entrance to Owl Wood we shall have to use the road. Not long after passing the East Riding Waste Recycling Centre, we arrive in Burnby.

St Giles Church should be open to visitors and, having admired the Norman carvings over the porchway, we should certainly go inside to see the fine Norman font. Leaving the church, we carry on round to the crossroads and turn left following the sign for Nunburnholme. It's a mile or so to walk and, though the map calls the slope 'Long Hill', it's only a gentle gradient.

If we did not visit St James' Church on Walk 7, we must make certain that we stop today because inside the building the Nunburnholme Cross is spectacular and the face carvings on the nave arch are superb. The church is 100m or so past the Wolds Way fingerpost and the church key is obtained from Rose Cottage on the other side of the road. When we have finished at the

church, we retrace our steps to the fingerpost directing us right on the Wolds Way.

We are now back on the linear route of the Wilberforce Way and for the next couple of miles the walk follows Wolds Way fingerposts and indicators, so there are no real navigation difficulties. After going round two sides of our first field, we turn left on Lowfield Lane and continue for 150m before branching off right up through Bratt Wood (4). On leaving the wood, we continue to Wold Farm where we bear left before going through the farmyard to come out on a tarmac farm drive. At a solitary house (5), we turn sharp right, then sharp left and come to the B1246 on Kilnwick Percy Hill. Crossing straight over, the trail continues over pastoral and then arable country to Low Warrendale Farm. We pass round the far side of the farmstead and follow the road, twisting down and up the steep sides of Warren Dale dry valley.

A little further on at the crossing (6), the Wolds Way turns right but the Wilberforce Way turns left. We stay on the open road, passing the drive to Kilnwick Percy Hall and then the entrance to Kilnwick Percy Golf Club, until we reach the signposted footpath at (7). Here we turn right. The p.r.o.w. crosses the golf course, swings left following the edge of Spring Wood and then goes between hedge and fence to the path junction at (8). About 20m after the fingerpost, we fork down left to the edge of the built-up area.

We cross one road, then at the second road turn left but, instead of walking on the road, use the Woodland Trust path through St Helen's Well Wood. Leaving the wood, we bear left on the road to come out at Woldgate College on the B1246. Here we go right and follow this road into the town centre. We arrive in the Market Place and have the chance to visit All Saints Church before returning via The Pavement and Railway Street to our start.

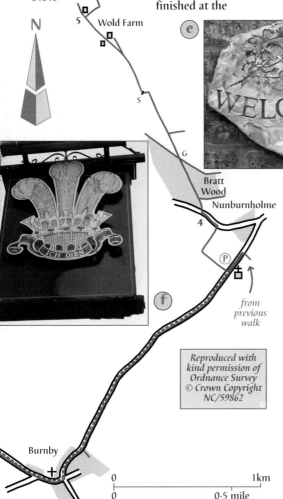

Low Warrendale Farm

B1246

N

Wold Farm

Bratt Wood

Nunburnholme

from previous walk

Burnby

0   1km
0   0.5 mile

WALK 9
POCKLINGTON -
MELBOURNE INGS

Map: Explorer 294
S.E.P.:   West Green car park (801488)
Bus: X46 to Pocklington bus station
                                 (803488)

Wilberforce Way distance:	**6.2 miles**
Circular walk distance:	**11.7 miles**

Special interest:
        Pocklington Canal SSSI,
        Allerthorpe Common, Allerthorpe
NB: In winter, check that the Canal path
        is not flooded. If it is, the cycle route
        can be used instead.

We continue to the Melbourne Arm (7), a docking station for barges, and note that from here the canal has been cleared for navigation downstream. A short way further on is the p.r.o.w crossing Melbourne Ings and at this point we turn right and leave the canal-side (8).

A good path is waymarked over farmland

As with Walk 8, the circular walk starts next to Pocklington School. We walk down Cemetery Lane, which is opposite the school, and go to the end of the road. Turning right, we use the path inside the perimeter of the cemetery (rather than the p.r.o.w. next to it, which can be overgrown) and go to the end of the older graves. We turn left and right around the edge of the newer graves and reach the gate in the cemetery corner at (1). A waymark directs us more or less straight ahead for about 200m along the left side of the hedge to the field corner at (2). The O.S. map shows the p.r.o.w. going diagonally left across the next field but when I first walked the route there were 2m high maize and sunflowers growing here, so I chose to keep to the field edge. Then going through the hedge to the left of the old Devonshire Mill, a lovely green path takes us to the A1079, but we must make sure we fork right over the stile where the main path swings left at (3).

At the main road we go right before crossing over to the Canal Head car park and picnic site at the start of the Pocklington Canal. We shall be walking beside the canal for a little over 5 miles on the present walk but there should be time to read the information boards before we continue. The going is easy and, if it is summer time, there's the opportunity to see how many species of dragonfly we can spot.

When we come to Coat's Bridge (4), we may choose to stay on the same side of the canal or to walk on the opposite (east) bank. If we do change sides, this will mean that at the drainage ditch (5) near Bielby we do a slight diversion but then can use the permissive path through the trees to the footbridge at (6). Here we cross back again over the canal.

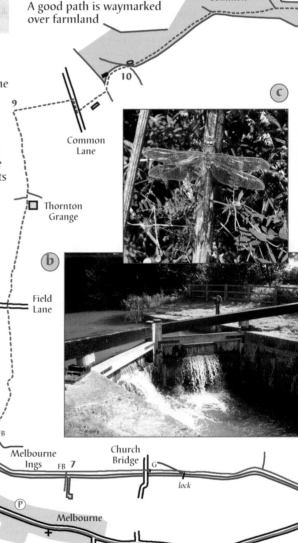

and, keeping to field edges, we cross Field Lane, pass Thornton Grange Farm, turn 90° at the field corner (9) and come to Common Lane. We go right for 80m before turning off along the path on our left. As we walk we'll probably hear the squeals of happy piglets to our right and then at the end of the first field the path swings left before curving round right to the opening into Allerthorpe Wood on our left (10).

We go into the wood and bend right. The next part of the walk offers a quite different

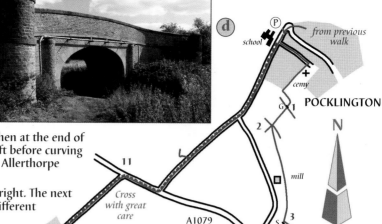

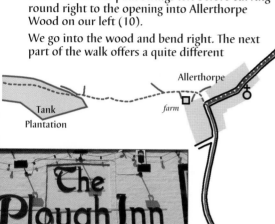

POCKLINGTON

N

A1079

Cross with great care

Allerthorpe

Tank Plantation

farm

Canal Head

Cross with great care

school

cemy

mill

lock

Reproduced with kind permission of Ordnance Survey © Crown Copyright NC/59862

lock

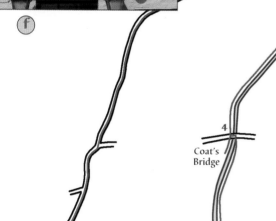

Pocklington Canal

leave the Forestry Commission property, the track continues through the deciduous Tank Plantation and then, after passing Manor Farm, becomes a tarmac surface bending right into Allerthorpe.

At The Plough pub we turn left and go through the village. We can look into St Botolph's Church before following the pavement to the A1079 (11). Crossing carefully, we go right for a short distance to Hodsow Lane and here turn left back to Pocklington. Fortunately there is a pavement all the way and we can watch the activities of the Gliding Club rather than having to look all the time at the traffic on the road.

Coat's Bridge

Walbut Bridge

environment as we enter the coniferous forest, developed on Lowland Heath habitat, and follow the bridleway just inside the trees. When we

POCKLINGTON - THE SCHOOL CONNECTION

He wrote his first public letter against the slave trade when he was a 14-year old at the school. Reverend T.T. Walmsley, a fellow student, said of Wilberforce: *'His abomination of the slave trade he evinced when he was not more than 14 years of age.... One day he gave me a letter to put into the post office, addressed to the editor of the York paper, which he told me was in condemnation of the odious traffic in human flesh'**. We are not sure if the letter was ever printed. It certainly would not have been popular amongst those whose wealth was dependent on the slave trade.

Pocklington School was founded by John Dolman in 1514 as a grammar school and is now a fee-paying boarding and day school with a strong Christian ethos. 'The Greatest Yorkshireman' was a pupil here for five years from 1771-1776. His agreeable nature and talent for singing made him popular and a former classmate recalled that he *'greatly excelled all the other boys in his compositions'*.

To mark the 2007 commemoration, the school is honouring Wilberforce's many achievements with a specially commissioned full size bronze creation by local sculptor Sally Arnup. However, in contrast with the statues in Hull, Cambridge and Westminster Abbey, the Pocklington statue is to be that of Wilberforce the schoolboy. The school also owns an oil painting of the young Wilberforce by the artist Arthur Devis. A picture of Wilberforce painted when he was eleven by John Russell is held at the National Portrait Gallery and can be viewed online (www.npg.org.uk).

(*Quoted in 'The Life of William Wilberforce' (Volume 1) by Robert & Samuel Wilberforce (1839))

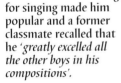

Clay model being prepared by Sally Arnup

SPECIAL INTEREST - **WALK 9**

Pocklington Canal is an important heritage waterway as well as a special area for wildlife conservation. The 9.5-mile long canal was built between 1815 and 1818 to join Pocklington with the River Derwent at East Cottingwith. Goods carried included coal, lime, fertiliser and roadstone for Pocklington and the surrounding area. Farm produce moved in the opposite direction for the industrial towns of West Yorkshire but traffic started to decline after the arrival of the railway in 1847. The last cargo was carried in 1932. Restoration of the canal began in 1969 and work to rebuild and maintain the locks continues. The four road bridges are Scheduled Ancient Monuments while 8 of the 9 locks are Grade II listed structures.

The Canal forms part of the extensive wetland region of the Lower Derwent Valley which is one of the country's most important wildlife conservation areas. Apart from giving habitat to a number of unusual aquatic plants, the Canal supports at least 15 species of dragonfly and damselfly. Of special importance is the red-eyed damselfly which can be seen resting on the leaves of the water lilies. Water vole and otter are known to be present.

Much of the canal, together with some of the adjacent ings, forms an SSSI. The 'ings' are seasonally flooded, traditionally managed, hay meadows of international significance. In spring and summer the fields provide home for hundreds of nesting wildfowl and waders – over 80 bird species are known to have bred here in recent years. Then in winter the same meadows support even greater numbers of wildfowl, including birds coming from as far away as Siberia. Teal can number up to 2,000 and wigeon up to 3,000.

Allerthorpe Common SSSI contains 'Lowland heathland', the kind of vegetation characterised by heather, oak, gorse and birch and usually found on poor, sandy, acidic soils. It probably did not exist in the Vale of York before Bronze Age settlers arrived about 4,000 years ago and cleared the land.

However, it is becoming clear that lowland heathland (or 'moorland' as it seems to have been locally known) used to occupy much greater areas in the Vale of York than it does today. Enormous losses have occurred and it is estimated that over 95% has disappeared. Now only a few remnants survive at Skipwith, Strensall and Allerthorpe. Nevertheless, O.S. maps still name numerous places in the region as 'moor' or 'common'.

'Commons' are areas where the population held common rights, usually for grazing animals or gathering fuel, and heathland, rather than forest, is thought to have dominated much of the landscape in the Vale of York. However, these old moors or heathlands were lost when they became enclosed and drained for improved farming in the time of the Agricultural Revolution (very roughly 1750-1850). Old maps show that between 1775 and 1855 about 80% of the once extensive Barmby Moor (which included Allerthorpe Common) had become enclosed.

Further reductions meant that in all 99% became lost. In the 1960s, for instance, the Forestry Commission planted extensive areas of Allerthorpe Common with pine trees so that heathland communities (heather, cross-leaved heath, purple moor grass and cotton grass) were largely confined to a 6-hectare nature reserve and an unplanted area in the north-east of the Common. A special feature of the reserve is the large stand of marsh cinquefoil.

Planning ideas have now changed and The Restoring the Heaths of the Vale of York Project is a programme designed not only to protect the surviving heaths but also to re-create heath on some of the land that had been planted with coniferous woodland. In the future it is possible that Exmoor ponies may be introduced to graze the heath. This would be done in order to stop taller species from taking over and smothering smaller plants.

Adders are found on Allerthorpe Common but they are shy and not regarded as dangerous unless interfered with by humans or dogs. Breeding birds include nightjar, tree pipit and whinchat. A recent exciting archaeological discovery has been the remains of what is thought may have been an ancient iron-smelting site, using poor quality material from the 'iron pan' found in the soil.

St Botolph's Church, Allerthorpe dates from 1876 and stands on the site of an earlier place of worship. There is documentary evidence of a church in the village as early as the time of Henry I (1101-1135) and some parts of the present structure, for example the internal chancel arch, may contain re-used medieval stones.

Reeds that fringe the canal and ditches hold increasing numbers of sedge and reed warblers and add to the variety of species present

(Note the distinctive eye-stripe on the sedge warbler. A good place to spot the warblers is around Coat's Bridge.)

Barn Owl
(length 33-39cm –
wing span 85-93cm)

Reed Warbler
(length 12.5cm)

Sedge Warbler
(length 13cm)

Kingfisher
(length 16-17cm - wing span 24-26cm)

Brown Hawker
Aeshna grandis
(length 73mm –
wing span 102mm)

Banded Demoiselle
Calopteryx splendens
(length 45mm – wing span 63mm)

Four of the fifteen species of dragonfly that frequent the Pocklington Canal

Terry Weston carried out a dragonfly survey for English Nature (Natural England) along the Pocklington Canal during 2003-2004. He identified 15 different species and generously agreed to include a selection of his photographs in this publication. Hot days in the first couple of weeks of July are probably the best time for seeing both dragonflies and damselflies. Look for them on the yellow water lilies.

NB: The images are not shown to scale.

Red-eyed Damselfly
Erythromma najas
(length 35mm – wing span 45mm)

Common Hawker
Aeshna juncea
(length 74mm – wing span 95mm)

WALK 10
MELBOURNE INGS – SUTTON UPON DERWENT

Map: Explorer 294
S.E.P.:   Melbourne village (745443)
Bus: Sutton upon Derwent Service 195 or
             196 (no Sunday service)
Wilberforce Way distance: **4.6 miles**
Circular walk distance: **10.4 miles**
Special interest:
             Pocklington Canal SSSI, Allerthorpe
             Common
NB: In winter, check that the Canal path
             is not flooded. If it is, the cycle route
             can be used instead.

The Wilberforce Way continues along the side of the Pocklington Canal as far as Hagg Bridge and then follows the B1228 into Sutton upon Derwent. From there the circular walk turns eastwards along Sandhill Lane to Allerthorpe Wood and then retraces, in the opposite direction, the paths used on Walk 9.

If we start the walk from Melbourne, we take the p.r.o.w. near the western end of the village (1) and cross over the canal to the point reached on the last walk. This time we turn left and stay by the canal-side for just over 2 miles until we reach Hagg Bridge. This stretch of the waterway has been cleared for barge navigation and so does not have the same choked appearance noted previously but there is still a wealth of birds, butterflies and dragonflies to catch our attention in summertime.

At Hagg Bridge we leave the footpath and come up to the B1228 (Common Lane). From here

into Sutton upon Derwent we follow a wide grass verge, and then pavement, until just after The Sutton Arms pub. The second turning on the right after the pub is Wynam Lane (2). Turning off here, a waymarked and signed path zig-zags

round field edges and brings us out on to Sandhill Lane (3).

Bearing right along this quiet road we pass the Woodhouse Grange Cricket Club. The club gained well-deserved attention when it won the national village cricket club final at Lords in 1995. Four years later the club again reached the final, although on this occasion was beaten into second place. A little further along the road we pass the carefully mown turf of Rolawn and then, just after the driveway to Allerthorpe Farm stud, come to Allerthorpe Wood. Ignoring the overgrown p.r.o.w. on our right, we continue for about another 100m to the FC track opposite to the

layby parking space on the left-hand side of the road at (4).

Leaving the road, we now follow the wide track through the trees, cross over Common Lane and continue to the track junction at (5). We turn right here, leave the trees and now follow in reverse direction the route we took on the previous walk.

Staying just outside the wood, we swing round left to the field corner at (6), bear right past the pig sheds, go right for 80m along Common Lane and then turn left at the fingerpost. The waymark at the end of the first field (7) directs us left; we pass Thornton Grange Farm, cross Field Lane, continue to the footbridge over The Beck, cross the canal and then walk back to Melbourne village.

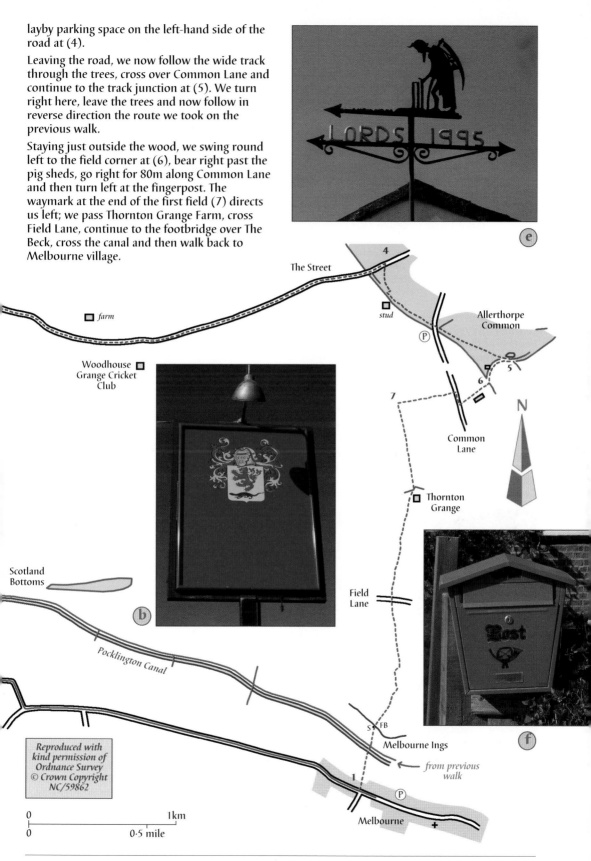

WALK 11
SUTTON UPON DERWENT – near POOL BRIDGE

Map: Explorer 290
S.E.P.: Wynam Lane, Sutton upon Derwent (708468)
Bus: Sutton upon Derwent – Number 195 or 196 (no Sunday service)
Wilberforce Way distance: **7.0 miles**
Circular walk:
It is difficult to devise a satisfactory circular walk
Special interest: Churches of St Michael (Sutton), Holy Trinity (Elvington), St Helen (Wheldrake)

This section of the Wilberforce Way involves a considerable amount of road walking and, because of the lack of inter-connecting paths, it is difficult to devise a satisfactory circular route. It is therefore recommended that this part of the trail be completed as a linear walk only. We start from Wynam Lane in Sutton upon Derwent. Here there is room for car parking and this is the point where the previous walk branched off from the B1228.

Going north through the village, we pass the St Vincent Arms pub, pause to visit St Michael and All Angels Church and then cross the River Derwent on the late 17th century Sutton Bridge.

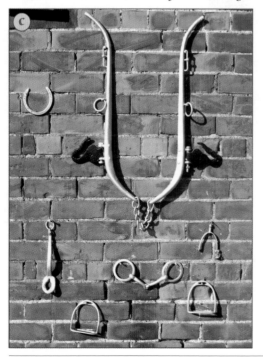

Immediately after the bridge, we double back on the p.r.o.w. on our left and soon bend round right beside Elvington Lock before coming to Holy Trinity Church in Elvington. Going through the church gate for about 20m along the path, we stop to inspect the gravestone on our left dedicated in memory of Fisher Murray, 'a faithful Black Servant'.

Leaving the church we take the road straight ahead to Red House Farm where we continue on the track bending left. After 40m we fork right at the fingerpost (1) on to a grassy bridleway. The route is clear as far as Cheesecake Farm but about 80m after the farmhouse we leave the main track where it bends right and we have to do a left-right shuffle in order to continue on the p.r.o.w.

At the next farm, Mount Pleasant, there has been a path diversion that takes us past the farm itself. Waymarks make the route clear and from the farm a broad track leads us out on to Church Lane and Wheldrake (2).

We turn right on the road, come to St Helen's Church and then a little further on, immediately after the pub, turn right down Dalton Hill (3). Then it's first left on North Lane (past the school on our right) and first right on Broad Highway. As the latter is a 'no through road' there's little traffic as we continue to Hagg Wood Walk (4). We turn left on the signposted, tarred path

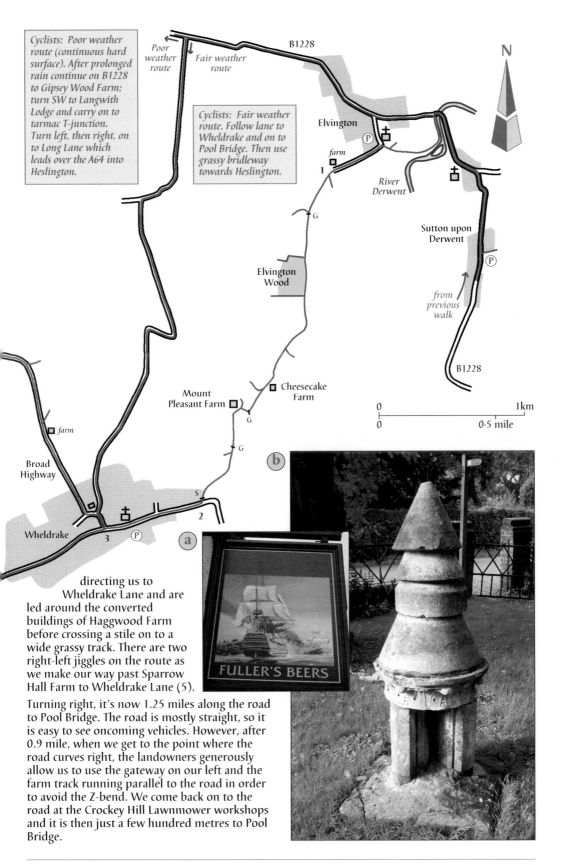

Cyclists: Poor weather route (continuous hard surface). After prolonged rain continue on B1228 to Gipsey Wood Farm; turn SW to Langwith Lodge and carry on to tarmac T-junction. Turn left, then right, on to Long Lane which leads over the A64 into Heslington.

Poor weather route

Fair weather route

B1228

Cyclists: Fair weather route. Follow lane to Wheldrake and on to Pool Bridge. Then use grassy bridleway towards Heslington.

Elvington

farm

1

River Derwent

Sutton upon Derwent

G

Elvington Wood

from previous walk

B1228

Cheesecake Farm

Mount Pleasant Farm

G

G

0   1km

0   0.5 mile

b

farm

Broad Highway

S

2

Wheldrake

3   P

a

FULLER'S BEERS

directing us to Wheldrake Lane and are led around the converted buildings of Haggwood Farm before crossing a stile on to a wide grassy track. There are two right-left jiggles on the route as we make our way past Sparrow Hall Farm to Wheldrake Lane (5).

Turning right, it's now 1.25 miles along the road to Pool Bridge. The road is mostly straight, so it is easy to see oncoming vehicles. However, after 0.9 mile, when we get to the point where the road curves right, the landowners generously allow us to use the gateway on our left and the farm track running parallel to the road in order to avoid the Z-bend. We come back on to the road at the Crockey Hill Lawnmower workshops and it is then just a few hundred metres to Pool Bridge.

St Michael and All Angels Church, Sutton upon Derwent has a fascinating history as outlined in the church information leaflet. A cross-shaft from Saxon times was discovered when a previously blocked Norman arch was opened up in 1927, suggesting that there had been a church here before the Normans arrived. However, the first recorded building on the site was a small stone construction, built about 1080 to 1100 by the de Percy family. This was later enlarged but when the Norman tower collapsed in the early 14th century, the church had to be almost completely rebuilt. Numerous other alterations have taken place since then and in 1927 a new vestry was added to the building. It was during this work that a body, believed to be that of Robert de Gloucester, the rector in 1234, was found together with his communion cup and plate. These articles are now lodged in the crypt at York Minster.

Walking around the church, we should look for the list of clergy who have ministered here since

1234; the stone carving dated from around 1340 and representing St George and the dragon; and the south wall log holes used by the builders for scaffolding during the 14th century alterations.

Holy Trinity Church, Elvington also has a long history. A church is recorded in the Domesday Survey of 1086 and, although there is no evidence of any dedication until 1287, the church retains its Norman font. Elvington's 'old' church was built in 1803 but had to be demolished and rebuilt in the 1870s a little to the south.

The churchyard contains a reminder of the 18th century practice of some wealthy Englishmen who brought home slaves from the colonies to work for them in this country. On his memorial gravestone **Fisher Murray** is described as 'a faithful Black Servant who came from Madeira with Thomas Cheap Esqr, who was consul there, and after living sixty years in the family died the 18th Dec 1821'.

St Helen's Church, Wheldrake is dedicated to the mother of Constantine the Great who was proclaimed Roman Emperor in York and who allowed Christians to practise their religion freely throughout the Empire without the fear of persecution.

A church at Wheldrake is mentioned in the Domesday Survey, though the village was then known as Coldrid. Unfortunately nothing remains of the Norman building. However, 14th century work in the tower can be identified by the smaller stones whereas the 15th century rebuilding work used much larger blocks. The main body of the church dates from 1778-9. The medieval font has been returned to the church after having been replaced for a time by a more modern one.

Heslington Tillmire is an SSSI developed on silt and clay deposits and is important for its marshy grassland. The tall herb fen plant community with its marsh cinquefoil, bogbean, cotton-grass and variety of sedges, is the only one of its type known in the Vale of York. The marshy environment gives habitat for a variety of wetland birds and up to ten species have bred in any one year. These include lapwing, snipe, curlew, redshank, teal, shoveler and pintail.

The University of York was founded in 1963. Students have come from all over the UK and from 100 different countries throughout the world. The University lake is its central focus and was the largest man-made plastic lake in Europe when it was created. It is home to a variety of wildfowl species and in recent years rarities such as black tern, white stork and bean goose have been visitors.

Wood Carvings by Bill Hodgson include *The Five Continents*, a bas relief cut from a diseased beech tree. Its companion carving, called *The Four Seasons*, eventually became too rotten to remain in place and had to be removed. *The Five Continents* sculpture symbolises the bringing together of people from all parts of the world and this is an important aspect of University life. One part of the tree reminded Bill of an elephant and this became the Asian continent. Australia is depicted by an aborigine carrying a woomera. An American Indian, supported by a bison and an armadillo, represents the two American continents while Europa leans on a bull. The strength and freedom of Africa are seen in female form as a slave breaks free from her chains of oppression.

The more recent sculpture, cut from an old oak tree, is a stunning chainsaw carving of 33 wildfowl spiralling into the sky. They represent the many birds on the University lake and reflect the diversity of humanity, striving for height and flight, and so the title of the sculpture is *Aspiration*.

Heslington Church is one of the country's oldest Anglican-Methodist partnerships. The Anglican building of 1857-58 replaced a medieval church on the same site and then in 1973 a major extension was added to the north side. The Victorian chancel with its mosaic floor and striking reredos of 1870 was left unaltered.

WALK 12
near POOL BRIDGE – WALMGATE STRAY

Map: Explorer 290
S.E.P.:   Wheldrake Lane (646461)
Bus: Wheldrake Service 18 (no Sunday
            service) or any Heslington service
Wilberforce Way distance: **4.3 miles**
Circular walk distance: **9.2 miles**
Special interest:
            Heslington Tillmire, University of
            York, Heslington village

This stretch of the Wilberforce Way offers a sharp contrast to the last few miles. After the tarmac and fast traffic of Wheldrake Lane we follow quiet paths at the edge of Heslington Tillmire and Heslington Common and then continue through The University of York. The University has a policy of 'open access' so that members of the public may walk through the campus and enjoy its very attractive layout. The Wilberforce Way takes advantage of this concession although if a large number of walkers intend to use the route at any one time, it would be courteous to confirm arrangements beforehand with the University (01904 430000).

track that runs parallel to Wheldrake Lane and leads to the lawnmower workshops by the farm before rejoining the road. We then continue to Pool Bridge (2).

At this point we leave the road and follow the p.r.o.w. running N.W. towards York. We walk for about 1.5 miles passing Heslington Tillmire and Heslington Common. Heslington Common forms part of the Fulford Golf Club's playing area.

When we reach the path junction immediately before the A64 (York Ring Road) we need to bend right and then curl round left (3) over the bridge in order to cross the road. On the other side, by the electricity pylon, we turn back right and follow the sign for The Outgang before swinging left on the field-side bridleway that runs parallel to the main road.

Some 450m later (4), we turn sharp left to follow the line of an old dismantled rail track along The Outgang. At the end of this track, by the children's play area, we turn right to join the road, go left, and then left again at the mini-roundabout to walk along Heslington's Main Street. Here we see how some of the buildings in the old village have been modified to help cater for the needs of the University. At the end of Main Street, we have the

For those using public transport, the number 18 bus service runs along Wheldrake Lane between Crockey Hill and Wheldrake. Those using cars can benefit from a kind agreement with members of the White family who allow parking at Kirkland Close Farm a short distance eastwards along the road from Pool Bridge. Please remember that, as always, this gesture in no way confers any general right of public access.

From the gateway where parking is permitted (1) day walkers are allowed to use the farm

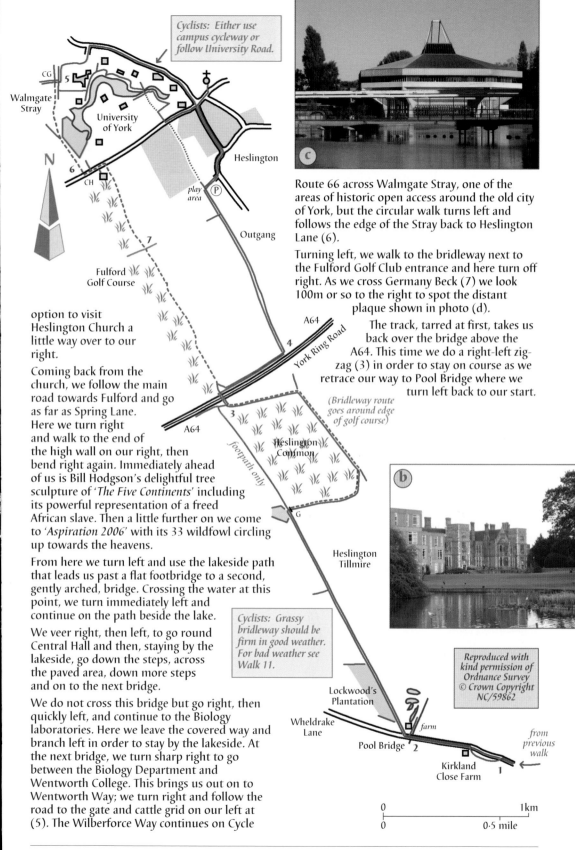

Cyclists: Either use campus cycleway or follow University Road.

CG
5
Walmgate Stray
University of York
Heslington
N
6
CH
play area P
Outgang
7
Fulford Golf Course

Route 66 across Walmgate Stray, one of the areas of historic open access around the old city of York, but the circular walk turns left and follows the edge of the Stray back to Heslington Lane (6).

Turning left, we walk to the bridleway next to the Fulford Golf Club entrance and here turn off right. As we cross Germany Beck (7) we look 100m or so to the right to spot the distant plaque shown in photo (d).

The track, tarred at first, takes us back over the bridge above the A64. This time we do a right-left zig-zag (3) in order to stay on course as we retrace our way to Pool Bridge where we turn left back to our start.

A64
York Ring Road
4

(Bridleway route goes around edge of golf course)

option to visit Heslington Church a little way over to our right.

Coming back from the church, we follow the main road towards Fulford and go as far as Spring Lane. Here we turn right and walk to the end of the high wall on our right, then bend right again. Immediately ahead of us is Bill Hodgson's delightful tree sculpture of 'The Five Continents' including its powerful representation of a freed African slave. Then a little further on we come to 'Aspiration 2006' with its 33 wildfowl circling up towards the heavens.

From here we turn left and use the lakeside path that leads us past a flat footbridge to a second, gently arched, bridge. Crossing the water at this point, we turn immediately left and continue on the path beside the lake.

We veer right, then left, to go round Central Hall and then, staying by the lakeside, go down the steps, across the paved area, down more steps and on to the next bridge.

We do not cross this bridge but go right, then quickly left, and continue to the Biology laboratories. Here we leave the covered way and branch left in order to stay by the lakeside. At the next bridge, we turn sharp right to go between the Biology Department and Wentworth College. This brings us out on to Wentworth Way; we turn right and follow the road to the gate and cattle grid on our left at (5). The Wilberforce Way continues on Cycle

A64
3
footpath only
Heslington Common
G
Heslington Tillmire

Cyclists: Grassy bridleway should be firm in good weather. For bad weather see Walk 11.

Lockwood's Plantation
Wheldrake Lane
Pool Bridge 2
farm
Kirkland Close Farm
1

from previous walk

0   1km
0   0·5 mile

WALK 13
WALMGATE STRAY – YORK MINSTER

Map: Explorer 290
S.E.P.:   Heslington Lane layby (618498)
Bus: FTR (Number 4) to University
Wilberforce Way distance: **3.2 miles**
Circular walk distance: **8.0 miles**
Special interest:
    York Minster, City of York,
    The Retreat

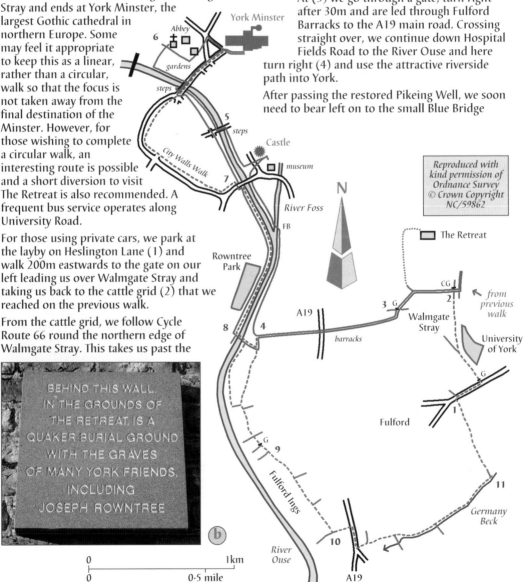

This final section of the Wilberforce Way continues from the eastern edge of Walmgate Stray and ends at York Minster, the largest Gothic cathedral in northern Europe. Some may feel it appropriate to keep this as a linear, rather than a circular, walk so that the focus is not taken away from the final destination of the Minster. However, for those wishing to complete a circular walk, an interesting route is possible and a short diversion to visit The Retreat is also recommended. A frequent bus service operates along University Road.

For those using private cars, we park at the layby on Heslington Lane (1) and walk 200m eastwards to the gate on our left leading us over Walmgate Stray and taking us back to the cattle grid (2) that we reached on the previous walk.

From the cattle grid, we follow Cycle Route 66 round the northern edge of Walmgate Stray. This takes us past the

boundary wall of The Retreat burial ground and on to the corner of the open land at (3). (Those wishing to visit The Retreat take the path on the right immediately before the allotments.)

At (3) we go through a gate, turn right after 30m and are led through Fulford Barracks to the A19 main road. Crossing straight over, we continue down Hospital Fields Road to the River Ouse and here turn right (4) and use the attractive riverside path into York.

After passing the restored Pikeing Well, we soon need to bear left on to the small Blue Bridge

Reproduced with kind permission of Ordnance Survey © Crown Copyright NC/59862

where the River Foss joins the Ouse. We continue to Skeldergate Bridge and, immediately after going under the bridge, cross diagonally right over Tower Gardens (the City's first public gardens) towards Clifford's Tower, the remnant of York Castle. The area between the Tower and the Castle Museum is known as the 'Eye of York'. This spot is important on the Wilberforce Way because it was here that William Wilberforce gave his Castle Yard speech in 1784.

Returning to the River Ouse, we carry on along the waterway to the King's Arms pub, climb up the steps at Ouse Bridge (5), cross the river and continue on the opposite bank along Riverside Walk. At the next bridge, we go under the archway, climb the steps and then cross back over the river on Lendal Bridge, before taking the steps down once more! Dame Judi Dench leads us past Museum Gardens and at the end of the Gardens, by the cobbles, we go right into Marygate.

We must make a quick diversion down the second turning on our left in order to see the memorial plaque to John Woolman at Littlegarth (6) and then we cross back to St Olave's Church. From here we take the path to the right of the church into Museum Gardens. Just after the museum building, we turn left on the path signed to the Minster and, on reaching Exhibition Square, we may wish to see the Wilberforce

'City Walls Trail' and follow the medieval walls past Micklegate Bar and round to Baile Hill (7). Descending the steps, we bear right, cross at the pedestrian lights and turn left down to Terry Avenue and the River Ouse.

Now we turn right and take the riverside walk (we can go through Rowntree Park for part of the way) to Millennium Bridge (8) and then cross to the other side of the river. Turning right, we go for nearly a mile towards Fulford. At first the path is still tarred but after passing the 'converted' church it becomes stony and then, forking left off the main track (9), it can get distinctly muddy! Here on the Ings was fought the Battle of Fulford in 1066. When we come to the path T-junction at a hawthorn hedge (10) we turn left and go up to the A19 road in Fulford.

We cross the road, turn right and then at Fordlands Road take the signposted Millennium Way footpath going left. This takes us alongside Germany Beck and, ignoring tracks leading off right, we come to the field corner at (11). We have to turn left and are soon back at Heslington Lane and our starting point.

plaque in King's Manor before going through the Bootham Bar archway and on to the Minster. We enter by the South Door and the Wilberforce memorial plaque is on the south wall of the nave just to the left of the information desk.

Those doing the circular walk leave the Minster and return, past the Dean Court Hotel, to the far side of Lendal Bridge. Here we join a part of the

The Eye of York is a dramatic site on the Wilberforce Way because it was here in the Castle Yard on 25 March 1784 that Wilberforce gave the speech that was to lead to his election as MP for the County of Yorkshire. He had been representing the City of Hull as MP since 1780, but had now decided to fight for the far more prestigious county seat, the largest constituency in the country and the one with the largest electorate. The meeting was called to give what was called 'A loyal address to the King' and to give support to the Prime Minister, who at this time was Wilberforce's close friend William Pitt. It would be a stiff challenge for the trader's son as he would be facing tough opposition from supporters of the landed aristocracy. Derick Bingham describes the scene like this:

Amongst the crowd that gathered to listen to the speakers were Lord Cavendish, his brother the Duke of Devonshire, Lord Surrey and the Earls of Effingham and Fauconberg. It was a cold, wet day and for five hours different contenders made their speeches.

When at last his turn came, Wilberforce got up and for nearly an hour captivated his audience. His charisma and the power of his oratory more than compensated for his insignificant stature. The biographer Boswell wrote:

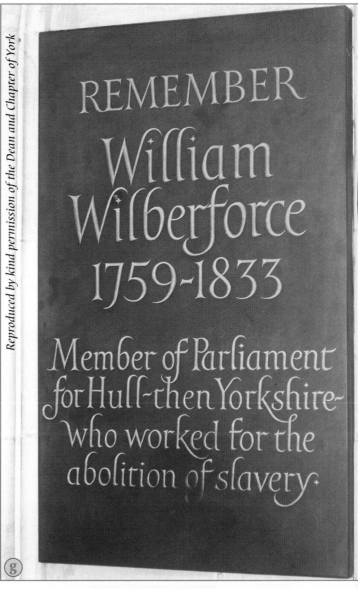

Reproduced by kind permission of the Dean and Chapter of York

I saw what seemed a mere shrimp mount the table; but as I listened, he grew and grew, until the shrimp became a whale.'

Suddenly, Wilberforce was interrupted. A King's messenger had arrived with a letter for him from the Prime Minister. Wilberforce read the message and announced the contents to the assembly: Parliament had been dissolved that very day and a General Election called! The crowd shouted their support and on 6 April William Wilberforce was elected as one of the two MPs to represent Yorkshire in the next parliament.

The Role of the Methodists in York

To many Methodists as well as Quakers, it generally went against the grain to become involved in what they regarded as the rather murky world of politics. However, in what is sometimes called the 'Politics of Pietism', if you could convince yourself that the matter under debate was a moral issue, rather than a political question, then it was justifiable to get involved. Both Quakers and Methodists were drawn into political action because they saw slavery as the great moral evil of their day and in 1791 The Methodist Conference promised its support for William Wilberforce.

It is worth remembering that around the time of the passing of the Abolition Act in March 1807, Wilberforce was in danger of losing his Parliamentary seat. Such was the anxiety of the abolitionists, that three circulars were sent out by the York Methodists 'to recommend to the friends of Mr Wilberforce to exert themselves in his favour without delay' and to increase their subscriptions for the coming election campaign.

The election took place in May 1807 and when the result was declared, Wilberforce had triumphed, Lord Milton was second and Henry Lascelles, a slave owner, had come third. Maldwyn Edwards writes: 'It is no exaggeration to say that a major reason why Wilberforce retained his seat was the untiring endeavours of Methodists in York to secure his election.' ('After Wesley' (Epworth 1935))

The Retreat lies at the north end of Walmgate Stray and is internationally important as the first community of its kind to welcome and treat as full human beings people suffering from mental disorder. Founded in 1796 on Quaker principles it emphasised the right of mentally distressed people to be accorded respect, dignity, privacy and freedom from fear. Unlike other 'asylums' of the time, it encouraged useful work, self restraint, a good diet, plenty of exercise and good relationships with staff as the means of recovery. The Retreat's early success rate led to much interest and subsequently other hospitals attempted to imitate its practice. Today The Retreat operates independently and uses modern, innovative forms of treatment whilst still maintaining the original Quaker ethos.

The Retreat complex contains the new York Quaker burial ground which includes the graves of Samuel Tuke and Joseph Rowntree. Visiting the site, we are moved by the simplicity of all the graves. There are no extravagant, ornamented tombstones; all have the same uniform pattern emphasising the Quaker ideal of every person being of equal worth in the sight of God.

Visits to The Retreat can be fixed by prior arrangement with the chaplain, Rev. Annie Borthwick (01904 412551).

The Role of the Tuke family in the anti-slavery campaign is interesting. William Tuke was the founder of The Retreat. His grandson was Samuel Tuke and in 1807 Samuel was so persuaded by Wilberforce's anti-slavery campaign that he spontaneously gave £50 (a considerable sum 200 years ago) from the family company towards Wilberforce's election expenses. But he did this without consulting his elders! His father, Henry Tuke, later wrote with considerable understatement: 'Samuel's bold stroke gave his grandfather and me some surprise ... Friends (i.e., Quakers) are generally disposed to discourage this kind of interference (in political affairs)'. Nevertheless, the family soon became convinced of the rightness of the cause and became actively involved in support of Wilberforce.

John Woolman was an American Quaker (1720-1772) who was passionately opposed to the evils of slavery. As early as 1756 he wrote: 'a neighbour desired me to write his will ... he told me to which of his children he gave his young Negro (slave) ... I wrote his will, save only that part concerning his slave ... then told him in a friendly way that I could not write any instruments by which my fellow-creatures were made slaves ... Then we had a serious conference on the subject, and at length, he agreeing to set her free, I finished his will.'

In 1772 he felt called to service in England but soon after arriving in York he was taken ill with smallpox and died at Littlegarth, in Marygate Lane.

Joseph Rowntree (1836-1925) has left a lasting legacy to York and as we enter the City we may recall some of his influence not only as a brilliant entrepreneur but also as an enlightened Quaker philanthropist. Developing a modest cocoa works into an internationally famous chocolate manufacturing company, Joseph Rowntree was a model employer. He wanted his money to be used to tackle the root causes of social problems, rather than just treating their symptoms. In 1904 he set up three charitable trusts, the most well-known being the Joseph Rowntree Foundation, as it is called today. The original purpose of this was to provide workers with good housing in the new garden village of New Earswick. The Foundation currently spends almost £10 million a year on its research and development programmes.

Those completing the circular walk pass Rowntree Park, a gift to York from the Rowntree Company.

St Olave's Church, York was founded by Earl Siward of Northumbria who was buried in the church in 1055. Then the building was given to Benedictine monks from Whitby and Lastingham who set up St Mary's Abbey next to it. The church was largely rebuilt in the 15th century and during the Civil War the roof was used as a gun platform, causing serious damage to the structure.

SLAVERY TODAY

Slave Raiding in the Sudan Baroness Caroline Cox has catalogued a heart-rending list of people she has met personally who have suffered from modern slave raiding in the South and West of Sudan. After the Islamist National Islamic Front (NIF) seized power by military coup in 1989 they quickly declared militaristic Islamic jihad against all who opposed them. One of the weapons they used was slavery and in a typical raid by government-backed militia the men would be killed and the women and children taken away as slaves.

The signing of the Comprehensive Peace Agreement for Southern Sudan offers a glimmer of hope that some of those enslaved in northern Sudan may be able to return to their homes. But their problems are enormous and any hope of a 'normal' life is unrealistic. The nightmares they had to endure as slaves will be with them for the rest of their lives.

Slavery Today – Bonded Labour in the Indian Subcontinent An article in *The Independent* newspaper* highlights the problem of 'India's shameful slave trade'.
Dev Lal is an escaped slave. He is also a Dalit – a member of the former Untouchable caste of India – and he was trapped into the vice–grip of bonded labour. Desperately poor, he and his family were tricked into accepting a job working far away from home in the brick kilns of Jammu in north-west India. The employers were unscrupulous and when some of the other workers ran away, Dev Lal was told that he was responsible for paying back their loans as well as his own. His wife and children would be held until the money was paid. Dev Lal escaped and then returned with Jai Singh, an Indian anti-slavery campaigner, only to find that his employer had sold his wife and daughters to other brick kiln owners but had kept his sons as hostages to try to force Mr Lal to pay off his 'debts'. Rushing to Kashmir, Mr Singh was able to release Mr Lal's wife and daughters. But the sons are still held. Bonded labour is illegal in India. The police have refused to help.

*The Independent 9 December 2006

Slavery Today - Trafficking in the UK In 2006, under the disturbing title of 'Bought and Sold in the UK', Amnesty International highlighted the following examples of some of those in the UK who have been caught in the trafficking nightmare.

Maryam was picked up by a trafficker and brought to London. Locked in a basement, she suffered repeated rape as a child prostitute. She was 13 years old. Six years later she was given false documents and finally let go. Trying to leave the UK, she was arrested, convicted and made to serve a 10 month prison sentence.

Theo was brought to Cornwall in February 2006 and set to work picking daffodils for major UK retailers. He was forced to work long hours, in all conditions for no pay. When he asked to eat, he was given dog food.

Jin Lai was 16 when brought from China to Kent. He was forced to live and work in a restaurant seven days a week to pay off a debt owed to the traffickers by his family. Without speaking English, he was helpless.

Pictured left:
Boy bonded labourer Pakistan (Sindh Province)
A person becomes a bonded labourer when his or her labour is demanded as a means of repayment for a loan. The person is then tricked or trapped into working for very little or no pay, often for seven days a week. The value of their work is invariably greater than the original sum of money borrowed. The United Nations Working Group on Contemporary Forms of Slavery estimated in 1999 that some 20 million people are held in bonded labour around the world.

Photo: Shakil Pathan/Anti-Slavery International

OUR RESPONSE – WHAT CAN BE DONE?

Our first response is to **become informed** and the following organisations are all involved in the anti-slavery campaign and can supply information:

Anti-Slavery International at
  http://www.antislavery.org

Abolish Slavery – Soon at
  http://uk.geocities.com/abolishslaverysoon

Set All Free at
  http://www.setallfree.net

Amnesty International at
  www.amnesty.org.uk

CMS at
  www.freeforalltour.info

USPG at
  www.uspg.org.uk

Christian Solidarity Worldwide at
  www.csw.org.uk

CHASTE
  (Churches Alert to Sex Trafficking Across Europe)

The second thing we can do is to **get involved**. The Act to abolish the slave trade 200 years ago required enormous investments of time, money and effort. It is possible for determined international pressure to persuade governments to change their policies and societies to change their attitudes. Individuals can play their part through letter-writing and campaigning. If you are not already a member, why not join one of the above organisations?

A third response is to **give generously** towards programmes that are working with the victims of slavery. For example, all proceeds from the sale of this book are being directed to programmes aimed at the elimination of child labour in India. One of **Christian Aid's** partners, **UPGSSS**, noticed how children of quarry

workers were having to work rather than go to school. UPGSSS now runs 15 learning centres and also helps parents to understand the detrimental effects of enforced labour on their children, depriving them of both education and the normal joys of childhood. The organisation lobbies for laws to protect children and supports families when they ask for decent wages and working conditions. The school in Fatehpur Sikhri caters for 185 children between the ages of 5-14 years. The children are either former child labourers or youngsters whose parents work in the stone quarries. UPGSSS believes that childhood should be a 'time to learn, not to earn' and this motto is inscribed on the clothes the children wear.

Photographer: Ramani Leathard/Christian Aid

The photo shows 12-year old Dharamvar at school. Until he was 10 years old he worked in the stone quarry and was paid Rs.20 (25p) per day. Now he is keen to learn and has ambitions to become a teacher. It costs just £2 per month for one child to be taught in an UPGSSS school.

One other response is to become involved with **Fair Trade** (see the inside back cover).

Bibliography

I have made use of numerous pamphlets found in churches along the route together with reference leaflets from Natural England (formerly English Nature), the 'Set All Free' campaign and information boards in several of the villages. Books deserving further study include the following:

D. Bingham, *William Wilberforce The Freedom Fighter* (Christian Focus 1998)		1 85792 371 5
C. Cox & J. Marks, *This Immoral Trade* (Monarch 2006)		1 85424 765 4
C. Emett, *Walking in the Wolds* (Cicerone 1993)		1 85284 136 2
C. Hill, *The Wilberforce Connection* (Monarch 2004)		1 85424 671 2
K. Jones, *The Saints of the Anglican Calendar* (Canterbury 2000)		1 85311 375 1
L. Markham, *Discovering Yorkshire's History* (Wharncliffe 2004)		1 903425 73 5
N. Pevsner & D. Neave, *Yorkshire: York & the East Riding* (Penguin 1995)		0 14 071061 2
S. Tomkins, *William Wilberforce: A Biography* (Lion 2007)		
John Wesley, *Thoughts Upon Slavery* (1774) – an early onslaught on the evils of slavery		

Churches in the following locations will be visited at the inauguration of the Wilberforce Way:

Walk number

1   Kingston upon Hull (St Mary) (Holy Trinity)
2   Beverley Minster (St John & St Martin)
3   Beverley (St Mary), Leconfield (St Catherine), Bishop Burton (All Saints)-cyclists only
4   Cherry Burton (St Michael), Etton (St Mary)
5   (no church on this section of the trail)
6   Goodmanham (All Hallows), Market Weighton (All Saints)
7   Londesborough (All Saints), Nunburnholme (St James)
8   Burnby (St Giles), Pocklington (All Saints)
9   Allerthorpe (St Botolph)
10 Melbourne (Methodist Chapel)
11 Sutton upon Derwent (St Michael), Elvington (Holy Trinity), Wheldrake (St Helen)
12 Heslington (Anglican-Methodist Partnership)
13 York (St Olave), York Minster

Photograph locations

WALK 1

(a)	The Deep	(103282)
(b)	Holy Trinity Church	(100285)
(c/d)	Mandela Gardens	(103288)
(e)	5 Scale Lane	(101286)
(f)	Argos reflection	(100285)
(g)	Land of Green Ginger	
		(099287)

WALK 2

(a)	The Ship	(073353)
(b)	View from bridge	(071354)
(c)	Wall plaque	(047391)
(d)	Old gateway	(046392)
(e)	Information board	(046393)
(f)	Notice	(056352)

WALK 3

(a)	St Mary's Church gate	
		(031398)
(b)	North Bar	(030399)
(c)	Pear Tree Cottage	(015435)

WALK 4

(a)	Entrance to village	(996421)
(b)	Entrance to school	(991421)
(c/d)	St Mary's Church	(981436)
(e)	Listed building, Etton	
		(979435)
(f)	Thomas Carling plaque	
		(979435)
(g/h/i)		
	House names, Main Street	
		(approx 978435)

WALK 5

(a)	Grannies Attic	(930439)
(b)	Wold Watch	(931440)
(c/d/e)		
	Kiplingcotes Station	(930439)
(f)	Hudson Way	(900426)

WALK 6

(a)	Nervous Pills	(890432)
(b)	Milepost	(890432)
(c/d)	All Hallows Church	(890431)
(e)	Rifle Butts Quarry	(898426)
(f)	William Bradley plaque	
		(876418)

WALK 7

(a)	All Saints Church	(869454)
(b/c/d/e)		
	St James Church	(848478)

WALK 8

(a)	Bloomsbury Cottage	(804488)
(b)	St Giles Church	(836463)
(c)	Throstlegate	(836465)
(d)	Hen and chicks	(836465)
(e)	Low Warrendale Farm	
		(832504)
(f)	Feathers Hotel	(804491)

WALK 9

(a)	Canal Head	(799473)
(b)	Sandhill Lock	(788457)
(c)	Camouflaged dragonfly	
(d)	Church Bridge	(758444)
(e)	Melbourne Arm	(753443)
(f)	Plough Inn	(783473)

WALK 10

(a)	Fingerpost	(747443)
(b)	Sutton Arms pub	(708466)
(c)	Fingerpost	(718476)
(d)	Beck Cottages	(725474)
(e)	Woodhouse Grange C.C.	
		(733472)
(f)	Silverhills Cottage	(740474)

WALK 11

(a)	St Vincent Arms	(707472)
(b)	Holy Trinity Church	(701475)
(c/d)	Mount Pleasant Farm	
		(691457)

WALK 12

(a)	Heslington Church	(628506)
(b)	Heslington Hall	(627504)
(c)	Central Hall	(623505)
(d)	Fulford Golf Course	(622495)

WALK 13

(a)	Memorial Seat	(617505)
(b)	Wall plaque	(617505)
(c)	Millennium Bridge	(603502)
(d)	Eye of York	(605515)
(e)	Jewish Memorial	(605515)
(f)	John Woolman plaque	
		(598522)
(g)	Minster Memorial plaque to William Wilberforce	
		(603522)